The Strawberry Lounge Story

How I got over my fears,
dumped my excuses and opened
the business of my dreams,
the Motherpreneur way

Christina Waschko

Copyright © 2014 by Christina Waschko
First Edition — June 2014

ISBN
978-1-4602-0371-2 (Hardcover)
978-1-4602-0369-9 (Paperback)
978-1-4602-0370-5 (eBook)

All rights reserved.

No part of this publication may be reproduced in any form, or by any means, electronic or mechanical, including photocopying, recording, or any information browsing, storage, or retrieval system, without permission in writing from the publisher.

Produced by:

FriesenPress
Suite 300 – 852 Fort Street
Victoria, BC, Canada V8W 1H8

www.friesenpress.com

Distributed to the trade by The Ingram Book Company

THE MOTHERPRENEUR

Mother: Look after, care for, nurse, protect

(Entre)preneur: businessman/woman (Oxford Dictionary)

MOTHERPRENEUR: A mother who uses her unique talents and passion to do what she always wanted to do and is living well because of it. ("Christinapidia")

For more information please go to www.christinawaschko.com

$1 from the sale of every book will go to YWCA Metro Vancouver, supporting a range of integrated services for women and their families.

TABLE OF CONTENTS

ACKNOWLEDGEMENT VIII
PREFACE XIII
INTRODUCTION 1
MOTHERPRENEUR IN THE MAKING 5
HOW THE IDEA WAS BORN PARADISE ISLAND / BAHAMAS 9
PART I **13**
MY PARENTS NEVER BELIEVED IN ME 15
BLAME IT ON MY CULTURE. 17
LIFE IS GOOD, WHY CHANGE IT? 19
I AM NOT READY YET 23
ONE MAGIC MOMENT 25
I HAVE NO CLUE WHAT TO DO 29
BUT IT IS NOT WHAT I DREAMED ABOUT. 31
I DON'T KNOW IF I SHOULD DO RESEARCH 35
BUT, I DON'T KNOW ANYBODY WHO COULD HELP ME. 37
I AM NOT AN EXPERT. HOW DO I BECOME ONE? 41
HELP. I DON'T HAVE A SUITABLE NAME FOR MY BUSINESS . . . 45
I CAN'T FIND A LOCATION. 49
IF NOBODY ELSE CAN, THE MAYOR CAN 53
I CAN'T TAKE IT ANYMORE 55
I DON'T HAVE ANY (ENOUGH) MONEY. 63
STAYING DEBT FREE. 67
SHOULDN'T I GET A PARTNER? 69
THIS IS TOO MUCH WORK 71
MARKETING? I HAVE NO CLUE ABOUT MARKETING.
HOW CAN I GET FREE PUBLICITY? 75
BUT, I AM NOT READY YET. I WILL EMBARRASS MYSELF 77
QUEEN'S DAY 81
THE FINAL COUNTDOWN - HELP, ONLY 6 MORE DAYS. 85
THE GRAND OPENING
THIS IS IT, NO MORE EXCUSES. 87
DAILY GRIND ONE BIG EMBARRASSMENT
HOW CAN I GET CUSTOMERS? 89

I HAVE NO CLUE HOW TO BUILD A BUSINESS	93
I CAN'T HOLD OUT ANY LONGER, EVERYBODY IS GIVING ME SHIT.	95
BUT, I DON'T KNOW ANYTHING ABOUT MARKETING. HOW CAN I REACH MY AUDIENCE?	101
I CAN'T WORK ON SUNDAYS, IT'S OUR FAMILY DAY.	105
WHAT IS HAPPENING?	107
I DON'T HAVE A USP (UNIQUE SELLING POINT)	109
TIME TO PARTY	115
ONCE YOU START THERE IS NO STOPPING	121
I KNOW NOTHING ABOUT HOSTING PARTIES	123
I HAVE NO CLUE HOW TO FIND GOOD STAFF	129
HOW THE HECK DO I DO INTERVIEWS?	131
HOW CAN I ASK FOR WHAT I WANT? ISN'T IT RUDE TO ASK?	135
SUCCESSFUL, HAPPY AND MAKING MONEY, WHAT'S NEXT?	139
TIME TO SELL.	143
PART II.	**147**
FAMILY AND BUSINESS DO(N'T) MIX	149
MY PARTNER DOESN'T SUPPORT ME.	157
MY CHILDREN ARE TOO SMALL. THEY NEED ME.	159
HELP, NO BABYSITTER AT HAND	161
PEOPLE STEALING FROM ME	163
WHY SHOULD I GO FOR IT?	165
WOULD I DO IT AGAIN?	167
HELP IN A NUTSHELL	169
REFERENCES: A CHECKLIST FOR SUCCESS	171
WORDS OF WISDOM.	173
MORE TIPS ON HAND	177
IN CLOSING	181
HERE IS THE NITTY GRITTY BIT: HOW I SET UP MY BIZ	183
THE BUSINESS PLAN	185
THE ABC'S OF STRAWBERRY LOUNGE	189
BIBLIOGRAPHY	191

DEDICATED TO

My parents Thurid & Sigi Waschko,
who taught me that living life on the safe side is good.
Therefore, I felt safe enough to do exactly the opposite.

And to

The four most important men in my life,
Dominic, Brando, Cohnan and Cruz.

ACKNOWLEDGEMENT

A heartfelt *Thank-you* goes out to everyone who visited and stayed loyal to Strawberry Lounge over the years. You guys helped to fulfill my dream and to keep the Strawberry buzzing.

The pages in this book simply poured out of me. The editing however did not. It goes without saying that the finished product was only possible with the help of Wendy Dewar Hughes at Summer Bay Press.

Thank you Harmony Cornwell for shooting this wonderful cover photo. I appreciate your time, patience and ideas.

Furthermore, it was a delight to watch how my friends from across the pond responded to my cry for help.

In particular, I wish to give a big imaginary hug to Anne Kuiper for making the drawing you see on this page; to Nanda and Kees Zwart who took so many pictures as soon as I asked for them. Linda and Richard, thank-you for sending more stuff in.

Brando, you are only fifteen years of age but unbeknownst to you, I promoted you from first-born son to my personal on-call assistant. You made sure that everything I copied, pasted and sent arrived at the appropriate pages.

My dearest sons, you were as patient as ever with me when I kept typing instead of joining the family entertainment program (yes, I did it again).

But most of all I want to express my deepest gratitude to Dominic, my wonderful husband and trusted friend for over 22 years. Dom, you are my savior. You were my rescuer when my innate German language was stronger than the English prose I wished to express. You are my knight in shining armor, always helpful, patient, full of inspiration and never too tired to explain the same process over and over again. You are simply the best. Thank-you for the hours we laughed together while reshaping the pages in front of us.

Thank you all for making "The Strawberry Lounge Story" come to life.

PRAISE FOR "THE STRAWBERRY LOUNGE STORY"

"I really enjoyed your writing. But most of all how you made me, as a reader, feel that I was part of your journey and experiences in the development and execution of your dream."

Colin Gerrard
Former CEO Granton Group, Producer, Director & Filmmaker

"This brilliant recollection from a courageous and honest writer will inspire and awaken dreams that lie dormant in the hearts of mothers around the globe. I read this story amidst a messy kitchen and sticky-jam toddler fingers, while the author led me on a journey far from my regular expectations as a mother. "The Motherpreneur" left me with an improved sense of family and dreams, and the possibility for the two to co-exist."

Jaci Botterman, mother of three children, Maple Ridge, BC

"The Strawberry Lounge Story" is the perfect roadmap, designed to help new entrepreneurs courageously leap into their business dreams.

Christina has outlined a blueprint filled with humour, inspiration and strategies that can bring you unprecedented success."

"The Strawberry Lounge Story" is a must in your library when you are ready to 'kiss your excuses goodbye".

Gail Vilcu
International Quantum Leap strategist
Greater Vision Accelerated Learning Academy

"This was a fun read about opening up your own coffee business which often can be a very competitive market. It shows you that you really don't need as much money as you think to compete but you must be creative and the author shows you how. If you ever had the dream to open up your own successful coffee bar (or any other business for this matter) but have been intimidated at the thought then this is the book for you."

Bob Burnham
Author of the #1 Amazon Bestseller:
101 Reasons Why You Must Write A Book: How to Make a Six Figure Income By Writing & Publishing Your Own Book

"Christina's book is the perfect example that you don't need to follow a system or a method to become successful in your chosen field. It is more about following your heart, your fun ideas and intuition. This is a fun & educational read. I loved it."

Troy Mobbs, CEO COBRA GROUP, Indonesia

PREFACE

My native language is German. For 12 years I lived in the flatlands of Europe, The Netherlands. Mix Dutch and German together, add English, (my husband's native lingo) and you will come up with an exotic mix I call "Dinglish".

As a woman and mother we are used to multi tasking; sometimes we succeed, often times we don't. When it came down to writing my story I was juggling with these three languages inside my head: I thought in Dutch, corrected it with German and wrote it down in English- can you see where this is heading?

I had such a hard time expressing myself in a proper, logical, and correct manner on these pages. My editor shook her head in disbelief when she read my Germanized English. I let her correct most of it; sometimes though, I thought it was much better to let the real Christina shine through. What I really want to say here is, brace yourself. At times you will read English the way I would say it in German. Or was it the other way around?

Before we get on with the story I need to get something else off my chest: Throughout the whole book you won't find the word "customer". To me, a customer is a nameless individual who does his shopping in a department store. In the hospitality industry we should refer to our paying customers as visitors or guests.

At times I refer to The Netherlands as *Holland*. Don't be fooled, both terms describe the same country.

INTRODUCTION

This is the story of Strawberry Lounge, a small, family-friendly, American-style coffee shop situated in Bussum, in the heart of The Netherlands. Strawberry Lounge never had the honour of being duplicated around the world, nor is it a multimillion-dollar business. Strawberry Lounge is the love child of a mother and her dream; conceived during a trip to the Bahamas, grown and matured during a 17-year-long gestation period, shaped and reshaped during a painful labour phase and finally delivered under the rainy, grey skies of the Netherlands; a far cry from its original plan, the Caribbean.

This is a story of a mother who faced her personal limiting believes, her fears, and her excuses to start her own business.

This mother is me.

I wrote my story with the idea in mind to inspire, motivate and encourage mothers around the world to do the same. Not necessarily to open up their own businesses but to follow their own personal dream. The dream we had before we became mothers, before we pushed the pause button and started raising our family. This has nothing to do with choosing between having children or having a career. My wish is to set an example and let mothers know, "Yes, it *is* possible." We can successfully fuse the mothers we are with the entrepreneurs we have inside us.

If starting your own business has never been your cup of tea then there is something else you have always wanted to do. Please, never stop believing in yourself or in your dream. Our children will always offer us plenty of perfect excuses not to do what we always wanted to do. The sooner we realize our children will always need us in one way or another, the sooner we can allow our children to become our inspiration as we show them a different side of their mother.

If however, you dreamed about opening up your own coffee shop, restaurant, or perhaps B&B, I want to assure you, ladies, there is an alternative to buying into the franchise trade. It is possible to start up, operate and run a profitable small business enterprise in the competitive world of coffee and espresso bars. I can also prove there is no massive start-up capital necessary to get you going. All it takes are balls (ladies, you know what I am talking about), the desire to be different, fun ideas, and quite simply, to follow your heart.

Strawberry Lounge never turned into another Starbucks and I am no Oprah Winfrey. On a personal level, I never had to rise above racial injustice, to struggle for survival, have never been through a nasty divorce, been diagnosed with cancer, or had a near-death experience.

I am a daughter, a wife and mother with three children. Being a mother has never been one of my sole priorities in life. Sure, one day I wanted to become one but foremost I wanted and needed to figure out who I am and how Christina could make the world a happier place.

Can you relate to these questions? Don't we all want to make a contribution to a higher course during our lifetime? Don't we all want to feel loved, valued and appreciated for what we are doing in one way or another?

We all have dreams, wishes and ambitions for our life. Some of them are big, crazy, and ambitious, others are low-key and toned down. Who is to judge? There is no right or wrong, big or small, ambitious or low-key dream. There is only one kind that matters: that it is your own.

My personal belief is we are much better mothers if we can somehow combine being a mother and fulfilling our own personal dreams. In the grand scheme of things, each of us has the opportunity to make the world a better place. If you are happy, your family is happy. Happy families make for happy communities, which in turn make for a happy country.

I want to share with you that it is possible to combine the mother and the dream-chaser you are. It is possible to start your own business with no formal education. It is possible to make money without having much of your own. The news of your business can spread without you spending time on social media. Your unique selling point can be as creative and crazy as you want it to be – just let it happen naturally. Starting your own business doesn't need to mark the end of your relationship with your family (yes, I am still married).

Okay, now here is a word of warning: Chasing ones dream isn't easy but it is worth it.

Success to me, is doing what you love doing and living well because of it.

Over the last twenty-six years I have lived in seven countries, on four continents. During that time I met not hundreds but thousands of women. From my conversations with the ladies, I realized we are all sitting in the same boat. In other words, we all want the same two things: We want to be loved, and we want to be happy. That means being happy with who we are, whom we share our life with and happy with what we are doing.

Here comes the crazy bit. For most of us it is not about becoming millionaires in our lifetime. What most of us want is to live a good and passionate life. If our chosen field happens to be a gold mine, so be it.

For the longest time I allowed my parents, my upbringing, my life, and then my children to be my excuses not to start my business. Finally something clicked inside my brain and I realized the fairy godmother would never appear into my life, swinging her magic wand around. The truth is, I am the fairy, and the magic is inside me.

When I started out, I knew nothing about business, absolutely nothing. All I had was my dream, my stubbornness, and will power.

As soon as you take matters into your own hands, when you break through the status quo and believe in yourself, you need to celebrate. Please read these pages as the celebration of an accomplishment. I am honoured you have chosen to be part of the party. May these pages inspire, motivate and be helpful to you, for one day I will be celebrating with you.

MOTHERPRENEUR IN THE MAKING

Ever since I was a little girl, I reached for the stars – metaphorically speaking.

My first career choice was to become a princess, none other than His Royal Highness, Prince Charles, the future king of England, was my chosen one.

Blame it on my good taste or a shift in my priorities but as soon as I became an avid reader and a movie fan, I wanted to become a screen legend. (Oh no, not just a normal actress.)

And last but not least, I decided to become an author. I fell in love with adventurous (and raunchy) books and I saw my future as a German Jackie Collins, ready to steam up my readers' bedrooms.

What can I say? Life doesn't always happen the way we want it to happen.

It seems as if life itself gets in the way of pursuing our deepest dreams and wishes. I am kind of glad it never worked out with Charles and me and am not disappointed my "acting talent" remained undiscovered. (There is too much attention on those poor actresses anyway. Who needs to look good all the time and is never allowed to stuff her face with cakes, candy and other necessities for life?)

Nope, so far I am happy with the choices I made.

And this book? One wish out of three isn't too bad, is it? Be warned though. While it might not raise your heart rate, it might inspire, entertain, and make you chuckle instead.

It seems like yesterday that I grew up in Kronshagen, a small town in the north of Germany. Everything was neat, safe, conservative, well thought through on my parents' part and nothing was ever spontaneous. If my parents had a say in my future, I would be married to our neighbour Hans, moved in next door and be living the exciting life of a civil servant with 2.4 children. Instead, I moved more than 10,000 miles away, married a "stranger" and have three children.

My younger brother and I surfed through our childhood on shallow waves. Our childhood was predictable, straightforward and protected by our hard-working, no-nonsense parents.

As soon as I finished high school a big empty void opened up in front of me and I had no idea what I wanted to do, become, study, or pursue. I had no idea what I was good at, what I was passionate about and what my life's purpose was. All I knew from an early age onward was that I didn't want to live in a small, or big, town in Germany. My "ambitious me" was looking for something different. What that was exactly, I had no idea. All I knew was, I wouldn't find it in Germany.

My parents' big dream for us was to find a well-paid job. A job meant a steady income, which in turn translates to security.

One of my greatest passions (and addictions) in life is exercise. I loved the idea of becoming a fitness instructor, however, most aerobics instructors I knew were university students and taught classes to subsidize their PE studies. Or they taught classes after they finished their 9-5 job. I didn't know what I wanted to study and I had no idea what kind of job I wanted to do. With this in mind, it seemed unrealistic to become a full time aerobics instructor when I first wanted to become one.

My parents wanted me to have a foundation. They wanted me to become a qualified *somebody* in any field so at least I had a foundation for a life in Germany.

After high school, I followed my father's advice and began a three-year apprenticeship with the biggest real estate company in our area. So here we have it, by becoming a qualified real estate agent under German law, I hit two rocks with one stone: I laid my requested foundation and my parents were off my back.

Holy Moly, selling houses was fun. However, sitting at desks in between got to me. After my three-year stint, I thankfully declined the company's offer to keep me on and decided to take on various, well-paid summer jobs instead. With my certificate in hand I felt so relieved and free. Now it was time to figure out what I really wanted to do with my life.

In my mind there was only one way to get through the early midlife crises: I had to put as much distance as possible between my parents and myself. Consequently, I boarded a plane to Melbourne, Australia. What was planned as a one-year trip turned into my "Quest of No Return".

Isn't it amazing how life unfolds when you are willing to take the first step into the unknown? Just let go and see what the universe has in store for you.

During my time Down Under, I met amazing people who offered me, among other wonderful opportunities, a job at a private boarding school in Florida. Another treat was to live on the Fiji Islands; and if this isn't enough, I met Dominic, the man who is now my husband.

In Australia, free from German constrains, I became an accredited fitness instructor.

My boyfriend, Dominic, worked for a massive direct-sales company at the time we met. He became one of their top salespeople and was offered work in England. This was totally to my liking and we spent a glorious five years in London. While Dominic was setting up offices, I taught myself branding and how to sell my services (a.k.a. fitness classes) to various fitness centers around the city. With my passion for exercise and my love for teaching, I finally figured out what I wanted to study. At the tender age of twenty-eight, I enrolled as a mature student at the University of East London and studied for my Bachelor of Science degree in Fitness and Health.

After living in England, we moved to Holland to set up another one of Dominic's enterprises. If you are not quite familiar with Europe's geographical layout, Holland is west of Germany, bordering the North Sea on the west and Belgium to the south.

Holland and Germany might be neighbors geographically, that doesn't mean we share the same culture or language. For one thing, the Dutch love their cheeses; we love our sausages. We speak German; they speak Dutch.

To speak their language is one thing, to write it is impossible (in my experience, that is). It is painful to admit but as a foreigner you will never get the grip on the pronunciation, only the Dutch can say words the way they are meant to be said. To make a long story short, my writing, reading and communication skills were limited. They existed but to the local ear I sounded like a third grader.

Holland was a foreign country for both my husband and me. None of us had any family ties or connections there.

In The Netherlands I started, ran and established Strawberry Lounge, the business that allowed me to call myself a motherpreneur.

After five and a half years in the business, I sold my "baby" and moved with my family to Canada where another part of my life was ready to unfold.

HOW THE IDEA WAS BORN
PARADISE ISLAND / BAHAMAS

Until my trip to the Bahamas, I really had no idea what I wanted to do in my life. I was floating through my twenties, living happily from day to day as a "suitcaser" in Australia. (No backpacking for me – a backpack was too small for all my stuff.)

Let me tell you briefly how my dream was born. In order to tell the story a bit better I need to ask you to close your eyes for a moment and picture the most perfect, serene beach scene known to man. If highrise hotels pop into view, you are thinking of Spain. Concentrate again, a little bit harder this time. Instead of Europe, think of the Caribbean. Let's think about palm trees, fine, white sand, endless beaches, turquoise blue water and luscious green. This is Paradise Island, a short flight away from The Keys in the south of Florida.

During my *quest of no return*, I was fortunate to meet up with my parents in Florida and together we travelled to Key West. For no other reason than fun, enough time and easy accessibility we flew to The Bahamas. Happily chatting, strolling along the beach, *it* came into view: A beachfront cafe.

The cafe was a simply built wooden structure, open on three sides. It had wooden tables, chairs, and colourful pillows to sit on. Their bright cotton sunshades were frolicking in the wind. There was absolutely nothing special or grand about it. It was harmony, blended perfectly together by wood, sand and water. Inside, the friendly, pretty, chatty waitresses were serving breakfasts with a smile and wearing only bikini tops and miniskirts. Behind the bar, a few drop-dead gorgeous young men were shaking up beautiful fruit cocktails.

Seduced by the location, the good-looking staff, their easygoing attitude, and an undeniable attraction to the lifestyle they represented, I found myself in love. Needless to say, we stopped to have a drink. Slurping on our alcohol free "Bahama Mama" it hit me like a hammer on the head: *Christina, this is it girl. One day you will own a coffee lounge on a sun drenched island.*

The idea of spoiling good-humoured, free-spending tourists under blue skies was exactly the vision I needed to get me through my early life slump.

Finally, I had a dream and a vision for myself. I locked this vision into my heart and labeled it "For one day in the future."

Little did I know it would take a long time, two house moves across two continents, a university degree, a career in the fitness world and three children later to finally live this dream – under quite different circumstances, I have to admit. In other words, I had lots of excuses before I finally made my move. And even then it wasn't what I wanted, really.

To this day, I have never set foot into a hospitality or business school. I am a big supporter and believer of the "University of Life". It teaches everything you need to learn about the most useful subject there is: Common sense.

If we want to get anything done in life we have to take action. We have to look our circumstances in the eyes and say: "Sod it, let's just do it.". Deep down we know the circumstances will never be right and the timing will never be perfect anyway.

You might recognize the excuses I used for so long before I finally kissed them goodbye.

PART I

MY PARENTS NEVER BELIEVED IN ME

My father showed me how to fill in a tax return. My mom taught me how to bake the most delicious fruitcakes. They both taught me about the rights and wrongs in life. My parents never taught me to dream.

This is the extent of my "personal torture" growing up. It was a safe, comfortable childhood surrounded by hard-working parents who made sure we lead a comfortable life in our small community. My parents never dreamed beyond our next holiday. They always worked. Immigrating to other countries was for hippies and losers. Starting your own business was for dreamers – way too risky, in my parents' eyes.

As soon as my teachers taught me to read I became an avid reader. With the help of books, I travelled the world and lived through many incredible adventures. Books made me want to see the world, rescue the good from the bad, and become a hero.

My parents, on the other hand, don't read. They read the newspaper and the occasional tabloid.

Any of my early attempts to share my future visions with my parents fell on numb ears. Neither of them had any idea what I was talking about.

Whenever I mentioned making the world a happier place, they ridiculed me. They gave me logical reasons why this was a dumb, unnecessary, fruitless idea. Everything I ever mentioned to them was answered with a big fat *NEIN* or a condescending pat on my head accompanied with the words, "Keep on dreaming".

They never ever gave me the thumbs up to believe in myself. In their eyes, I wasn't good enough (to move abroad), clever enough (to go to university), talented enough (to become an actress), or not tall enough (to be a model). They came up with excuses like, "You are a girl" (wearing baggy trousers), "We don't have enough money" (for you to go to boarding school), or, "You will never get this job" (when I wanted to become a stewardess).

I was alone with my wishes, dreams and hopes for a future outside Germany

Looking back, my parents always did what they thought was best for my brother and me. They always wanted to protect us from something or someone. Did they fear we might be disappointed or crushed when our dreams didn't turn out the way we pictured them?

The bottom line is, my parents did their best to discourage me in anything I ever wanted to pursue.

BLAME IT ON MY CULTURE

I am pretty sure the whole world is making fun of us Germans. Come on, be honest now, you know we are always on time (or try to be) and we are working hard. You picture us as the Bavarians wearing Lederhosen and playing in the Umptata Band. You also know we could commit a crime if we can't get our Sauerkraut, curry sausages or beer. You probably describe us as proper, orderly, well-educated, neat and well-dressed. In general, Germans colour inside the box, hardly ever outside the lines.

"Crazy, entrepreneurial go-getters" is not the phrase you would use to describe us. It was definitely not in the decades back when I grew up. Doing crazy, stupid things was for the Americans. The few brave ones who went against the grain were called *Aussteiger* (hippies of some sort).

During my teenage years in the 70s I read articles in women's magazines that favoured the young ones. Their message went like this: "When you are in your twenties, decide what you want to do in life. Find your partner and have your children not later than at the beginning of your thirties. Reap the rewards of your hard work when you are forty.

Don't bother starting anything new at that age because by then you will be over the hill."

This was the culture I grew up with. Thinking or doing anything outside the norm was frowned upon.

LIFE IS GOOD, WHY CHANGE IT?

As I wrote earlier, we need to get off our butts to make a change happen. It's all well and good to keep on talking, hoping, wishing and praying for something to happen but nothing will change if we don't take action. Eventually, it will lead to anger and frustration because we don't take any steps to make what we want a reality. We can spend lots of money on seminars, workbooks, mentors or coaches, yet if we don't do what they suggest then all that money is wasted. And let me assure you, taking action is difficult, especially if you have a fun job and your life is going well. Sometimes, it takes a tragic accident to make a change and to get into gear. Sometimes, it doesn't take a tragic moment to make a shift. Sometimes, it is a magic moment you experience. And sometimes it is fear.

Yes, you heard me right. My prime reason to start my coffee shop was fear. I was afraid of becoming too old to do it. I was thirty-nine years of age when the voices in my head became so prominent and so nagging that I stopped and took notice of my life.

We lived in Bussum, a small town in the middle of the Netherlands. My husband and I established our new life with our now three children in Holland. I was still teaching aerobics classes and life was sweet. Being a mother was fabulous, my classes went well, and we sailed through our live with full-blown sails. Life was good and predictable. I still had my dream but I was getting older by the minute. What happened to me? It seemed like I only recently left Germany but what had I done in my life? What happened to my coffee shop? I came up with my perfect excuse for not moving forward. I wanted to own a coffee shop on a Caribbean island, not somewhere in a small town somewhere in Holland. So, I blamed my husband for not making my dream come true.

But I was afraid of getting older, plain and simple.

"You are too old" are the most dreaded words someone can say to me. It is not so much the fear or worry of getting older; it is more the fear and worry that I won't have the energy, motivation or health to do what I still want to do at an increased age. Ladies, can you relate with this one? Is getting older one of your *worries*? Having a few wrinkles is not what I am talking about. The few laugh lines are signs of a fun filled life. But it is the unstoppable clock that freaks me out.

It was the artificial fear of getting too old to start my enterprise so late in life, the fear of "losing my edge" (if I ever had one) and fear of not being trendy enough to appeal to a wide range of visitors in a coffee lounge that stopped me.

I knew that if I really wanted to start my own business, I had to part with one of my life long passions – exercise. I needed to say good-bye to the aerobics floor, hang up my spinning shoes, store away my much-loved kick-ass music CDs and start fresh.

Fitness and exercise is my second biggest passion in life after my family. It always has been. For thirteen years I got paid for whipping other fitness enthusiasts into shape. I got paid for something I really, really loved doing.

Was being a passionate instructor just another excuse for not doing what I wanted to do since I was twenty-three? How could I give up what I enjoy so thoroughly? I worked so hard to become as good as I became. I devoted thirteen years to being who I was as an instructor. I built my reputation and earned good money with it.

How could I just stop and start fresh, in a totally new industry, in an industry about which I had no clue and no qualifications?

I needed a good chat with myself. Yes, I was good, and yes, I earned money. I never wanted to own my own gym and I knew: It was time to quit. Deep down I knew I wasn't as motivated as I had been when I had started out. More and more, I found myself teaching classes more for the money than for enjoyment. That, in itself, was a clear sign to stop. I made it so far into my career without getting a serious injury or without somebody calling me out of touch or commenting on my advanced age.

I AM NOT READY YET

At the age of twenty-three, I knew I wasn't ready to start a business.

When we moved to England, I finally figured out what I wanted to study. Going to university was my perfect excuse not to start a business. By the way, did I mention the exorbitant rental prices for property in London?

And finally, here is a real good excuse: I got pregnant. We were having our first baby. There was no time to start a cafe in between having morning sickness, getting bigger, having the casual afternoon sickness and not being able to sleep. Being a first-time mother took devotion, time, patience and lots of new things to learn.

Then along came another good excuse: I got pregnant again. Big cheers, we were having another baby. By that time we had moved to Holland and created a whole new life for ourselves. Ladies, do you remember how your second child changes the whole ball game once again? Having your first child needs adaptation, having two kids is a bit more demanding still. Start my own café now? You must be joking. I still loved teaching classes and our two children made for hectic living.

Then, oops, we did it again. I was pregnant for the third time. After the joy of having another baby, I realized one thing. I had mastered time management. Our oldest son had to go to school, the second one had to be dropped off at kindergarten and the third one needed to be entertained. In other words, I was on the bike (Dutch moms' primary transport) for too many hours to even think about my own enterprise.

And last but not least, I could blame my husband. He moved us to the Netherlands, the flatland of all European countries – the cheese-making, clog-wearing capital of Europe – and not to an idyllic, sun-baked Caribbean island.

ONE MAGIC MOMENT

Sometimes, we need to experience the tragic to create the magic in life. Thankfully, I needed one magic moment to help me make the decision to change the direction in my life.

Let us move forward to my fortieth birthday. If turning thirty wasn't bad enough, I promised myself to make the upcoming big birthday bash the beginning of a wonderful decade. We needed a real topper to mark my entry into official midlife. Dominic and I decided to climb a mountain – not a symbolic one, a real one. We both decided to hike to the top of Mt. Kilimanjaro in Tanzania, at 5895 meters, the highest freestanding mountain in the world.

The climb was an ordeal, to say the least. The hike itself was not difficult, what makes the trail challenging is the change in altitude. What you lack in oxygen, the path makes up for in breathtakingly beautiful scenery along the way. Our days were spent hiking; the nights were spent reading in our tent. At our arrival at the airport, right before departure, I had picked up the book *Anyone Can Do It,* by Sahar and Bobby Hashemi.

What were the chances that I would pick this one from all the thousands of books on offer? This book is written by the founders of *Coffee Republic* in England and was my sole nightly entertainment on the way to the top. The headlamp on my head burned holes in the pages. Their book intrigued and inspired me so much, I couldn't put it down.

The idea of opening my own coffee bar became more realistic with every page I read. The thin air added to my decision-making process. Somewhat delirious, I vowed to Dominic, "If I can get to the top of this mountain, I can definitely start and run my own coffee lounge." All that was left to do was to get to the top...

Ideas and inspiration started to pop up throughout our hike. The scenery even made me come up with a name for the future enterprise:

RUBICON CAFE Simply Great Coffee & More

Finally, on the sixth day, we reached the summit. Standing on top of the highest mountain in Africa is a feeling hard to describe. Deprived of oxygen, tired and exhausted, I felt sick, and my legs were shaking. Nonetheless, I personally have never seen anything as spectacular as this sunrise over the crater of Mt.Kilimanjaro. It is pure magical, breathtaking and beautiful.

Holy Moly, standing on top of Africa gave me wings. Yes, I was euphoric. Yes, I believed anything is possible in life if you only wanted it badly enough. Hadn't I just climbed six hours straight at a 90-degree angle to the top? Hadn't I just thrown up several times along the way? Hadn't I just forced myself to go on and on in the bitterly cold morning air, with freezing hands and the smell of vomit in my mouth? I believed in myself and I pushed farther and farther as we succeeded to reach the summit. Standing on top of Mt. Kilimanjaro was my magic moment; it was my personal shifting point from dreaming to doing. Here is the equation I came up with:

- Reaching the summit = Having enough stamina to open a coffee bar.
- Giving birth to three children = Having enough strength to pull it off.
- Receiving university degree = Showing determination and perseverance.
- Running a marathon = Being serious and prepared to succeed. (This mega run happened sometime in between having baby number two and baby number three.)

Finally. I had the guts to turn my dream into reality. Isn't it amazing?

So many of us imagine and dream about opening up a coffee shop, a restaurant, a bakery or a B&B and so few of us are doing it. Throughout my first year in business, I heard the following comments a lot:

"I am glad you have opened up, Bussum needed something like Strawberry Lounge."

"I've always wanted to do something like this."

"Are you interested in partners or franchising?"

Women made these comments, women of all shapes and sizes, various ages and backgrounds.

Over the course of my first year in business I built a very good rapport with one of our lady guests in particular. We started dreaming together. She wanted to become my partner to set up Strawberry Lounge within a bookstore in one of our adjacent towns. This lady made inquiries about our possibilities; she did her research at the city office for licensing and was calculating her finances. Unfortunately, she quit when the first obstacles appeared. In our case it was a lack of support from the town office and an impending split from her husband. Another dream vanished.

I HAVE NO CLUE WHAT TO DO

What were the steps I needed to take as soon as we got home? Normally, you should sit down and write a business plan. What did I do? I met with Chander, a graphic designer and printer, one of Dominic's business acquaintances. Together we designed the first Rubicon logos.

The original idea for Rubicon was a shop painted in orange, with blue, red and white serving plates and cups. These colours represent my then country of residence: Orange is Holland's national colour. Their then monarch, Queen Beatrix, belongs to The House of Orange-Nassau. On the other hand, the Dutch flag bares horizontal red, white and blue stripes.

BUT IT IS NOT WHAT I DREAMED ABOUT

Will you agree with me when I say *there is never the right time or circumstance to do anything in our life*? If we wait for the right moment, we can wait forever. It is up to us to create the right time and circumstance in our life, and what better time than now to get started?

Sometimes, a perfect situation looks us right into the face but we don't want to see it because it is not what we dreamed about. The Netherlands, living in Bussum was not what I dreamed about, ever. My bucket list doesn't even mention the word, Holland.

Bussum wasn't my perfect location. Bussum is neither an island nor a thriving tourist community. Here, the sky is more grey than sunny. Concrete grey or red bricks substitute for the luscious green of the tropics. Instead of a sandy path leading towards my front door, one walks on asphalt, concrete, or cobblestones. Whereas the beach cafe would offer serenity by looking out into the blue of the ocean, Bussum offers distraction by watching pedestrians or cyclists moving past.

As if this wasn't bad enough, Dominic made it crystal clear we weren't moving to the Caribbean soon (if ever). What needed to be done? I had to adapt the original plan to a user-friendlier, more realistic version, of what was possible.

What the heck...I had waited this long in my life. Instead of bringing Holland to the Caribbean, I decided to bring the Caribbean to Holland.

Adapting to my surrounding was one thing but I didn't want to adapt my menu. Rubicon had to become an American-style coffee lounge. I simply loved the idea of serving New York-style bagels, cheesecake, carrot cake, muffins and chocolate chip cookies. These products were different enough to make my coffee shop stand out from the crowd. To make it even more special, I promised to make my serving sizes bigger than anyone else's (which is not hard to do as most of the local servings are tiny).

Now, you might ask yourself, why wouldn't a true-blue German, who speaks with a German accent and thinks like a German (big portions), sell German cakes and German coffee? This is a good question and here is a perfectly good answer: This option didn't make sense. It's not that cakes from my home country are less delicious than their American counterpart. On the contrary. For my purposes they were just not special enough.

It takes less effort to hop over to Germany to stock up on cakes made in Germany than flying across the Atlantic to purchase "Made in USA". Furthermore, "US-style Coffee Lounge" had a better ring to it than "Deutsches Kaffee Haus".

We were parents first and business people, second. Choosing Bussum as location made perfect sense to us. We wanted and needed to be close to our boys. In case of an emergency or sickness, we needed to be back home as fast as possible.

Traffic jams can become quite ferocious in Holland. The plan was to operate within bicycle distance from our home and schools. What a luxurious way of life, I hear you sighing. The idea of cycling to and from work may sound weird to anybody out there living in a much bigger, hillier and more diverse country than the Netherlands. Rest assured, this is not as crazy as it sounds here in Holland. This country is small, flat, and populated by sixteen million bicycle enthusiasts. It is quite a sight to watch the local work force out and about, cycling to their respective offices or the train station – in their best business attire – suit, shirt, tie, skirts and high heels (though not necessarily all on the same person).

When we became parents we realized not all hospitality venues welcomed children and we saw a gap in the market. I wanted to create a nirvana for parents and their offspring but welcoming the childless population as well. I wanted to create the *Cheers* of our community. Do you remember this TV show with the wonderful slogan "where everybody knows your name"?

Footloose and fancy-free in the sun turned into family-oriented under mostly grey sky. I surely had come a long way. This is what children do to you – they make you change your whole plan. When you look on the bright side, this change of plan wasn't too bad after all. My children made me an expert in the field of parenting. Opening up a family-friendly coffee bar was the perfect opportunity to take advantage of my new found expertise.

For the sake of my future young and clumsy visitors, all my furniture needed to be easy to clean and cozy at the same time. The US-style cakes and coffee had to be easy affordable and would be served on a quirky mixture of plates. We would have lots of glossy magazines to flip through and music playing in the background.

If you research bistros, cafés or espresso bars around the world you will notice one common characteristic – they charge big prices for small portions. To this day I don't understand this concept. Tiny portions should be expected from a restaurant with a Michelin Star, not from the espresso bar around the corner. Owning my own coffee shop would be the perfect opportunity to show my guests what real value for money was. And while we are on the subject, why do so many individuals believe only expensive, small pieces of cakes represent real quality cakes? Where does this nonsense come from?

There was only one equation I knew about. In order to make money I needed either repeat business or a super-expensive product to sell. My housewife brain decided to make the core products, coffee varieties, easily affordable. I wanted and needed our guests to come in as many times as possible during the week.

Family and child-friendly go hand-in-hand with a smoke-free environment — not necessarily common in Holland. During the time of setting up my business in 2005/2006, it was still standard practice to smoke in the whole hospitality industry.

Another item I was missing was coffee made with fresh milk. Most restaurants or cafes in the area opted for using long-lasting milk and a fully automatic coffee machine. These machines represent a one-push operation. It is an easy and fast way to produce a cup of coffee but where was the fun; where was the creativity? Where were the passion and your skill as a barista?

To make matters worse, the coffee drinking public in Bussum was accustomed to this awful tasting brew so for the sake of having better tasting coffee alone I had to open a coffee bar.

I DON'T KNOW IF I SHOULD DO RESEARCH

We never conducted proper research to figure out what was missing in Bussum. We lived there long enough to know what we, as a family, were missing to make the town more attractive. No pedestrian counting for us either. It is not hard to figure out that a High Street is busier than the adjacent side streets or any streets on a *B* location.

What we did instead was quite simple. We, as parents, put our own wishes and demands on the list for a coffee shop and somehow knew we would hit the jackpot. Naturally, we visited bistros here in Bussum and in neighbouring villages. Unfortunately, everything we encountered was standard and similar – black coffee, apple cake, cappuccino, sandwiches with cheese, salad and cheese, double cheese, soups, ciabattas with cheese, salad and cheese, double cheese and more cheese.

Wasn't it risky to offer something totally different to my visitors? Of course, it was. There is a fine line between offering your visitors what they want and what you want them to experience.

In Europe, people love to travel. Regardless in which country you live, you are only a hop, skip and plane ride away from a totally different culture. The Dutch are no exception. They love to travel around the world. I made the big assumption many knew about and tasted cheesecake or carrot cake before and would be happy to find it in their own town. Yes, big assumption. Just because somebody has heard about cheesecake doesn't mean he will order it.

Looking back it was quite comic, really, how many of my early visitors refused to eat these cakes. Why? They all believed these were hearty cakes.

We are all creatures of habit. We like what we like and don't necessarily want to try something new – especially if it's cake that involves cheese or carrots.

What did I do? I simply force fed every new guest with sample pieces. Free, tasty samples definitely did the trick. Finally, my cakes got discovered and became famous. We gave out so many sample pieces at the early stages that later on I often didn't order enough cakes to keep up with demand. We only know what we know until something new comes along.

One tip from me to you:

Believe in your product. Don't get discouraged. Give out samples.

BUT, I DON'T KNOW ANYBODY WHO COULD HELP ME

It is so much easier if you have a mentor to guide you through the early stages of your upcoming business venture. It is even better if one of your friends, colleagues, or acquaintances is involved within your desired industry. Yes, life is so much easier if you surround yourself with people who are already doing what you are about to start. It is so helpful to have somebody to whom you can go for advice, information, or tips.

Unfortunately for us, we didn't know anybody who worked in the hospitality industry. There was nobody to ask for personal advice or tips and tricks of the trade.

The only hands-on experience or training I ever received came from summer jobs during my teenage travel and backpacking years. I worked for short periods at hotels, bars, cafes or restaurants. The only bookkeeping I ever did was long forgotten. I had no idea about price-margin calculations either. Product placement or best ways to advertise were all foreign to me, too.

My first hand experiences and knowledge came from being a housewife. (How and where do I shop for bargains?) Time management skills came from hands-on experiences as a mother. (What and how much can I get done while the baby is sleeping?) By delegating chores to my husband, I practiced management skills. Instead of a formal hospitality education I hold a diploma in self-belief and a deep desire to succeed. That should count for something, wouldn't you agree?

The only practical advice I ever received came from my father. Whenever we were in a restaurant he would tell us, "Go and check out the bathrooms. If the WCs are clean, the kitchen will be, too."

To this day I don't know if this is an old wives' tale or if my dad made it up. For the sake of argument I will give him the benefit of the doubt. Don't you just love this equation? I do, it makes perfect sense and goes hand in hand with my cleaning fetish.

My husband makes a living by talking. When he is on a roll there is no stopping him. Thanks to his verbal abilities I got in touch with a very successful restaurant owner in Amsterdam named Tom, and two Canadian coffee-lounge owners in Amersfoort, another Dutch city. Thanks to these three gentlemen I received my first useful information, requirements and tips on what to do and how to do it.

Tom offered these tips and information:

- If you want to serve alcohol you need to have a diploma in "Social Hygiene".

- Offer simple choices.

- Keep the opening hours consistent and easy to follow.

- Have your lounge open before everybody else does.

- Don't buy expensive furniture.

Thanks to Tom I enrolled into a self-study course for "Social Hygiene" at the Open University of Amsterdam. With a dictionary at hand I studied for months for the test, and passed.

The Canadian guys followed with:

- Keep the work floor clean, especially if you operate from an open kitchen.
- Be present on the floor all the time.
- Have a story to tell. Take advantage of the fact that you are a foreigner.
- Find your own USP (Unique Selling Point).

To me, these were nuggets. This is logical, easy-to-follow advice which I adopted from day one on onwards.

I AM NOT AN EXPERT. HOW DO I BECOME ONE?

I am a mother. Ask me anything about nappy-changing techniques. Ask me about how to teach a perfect aerobics class and I will give you answers to both of these questions.

I knew nothing about the coffee industry or how to make a perfect cappuccino. My passions are people, to laugh, connect and spoil them. My passion is not coffee. It has never been my dream to create an irresistible new coffee brew, nor was it in my head to sell the most amazing coffee made from expensive or unusual coffee beans from around the world. It was much simpler than that. I wanted to create the ultimate *feel-good coffee bar*.

From my experiences in the retail and hospitality industries, I know it is not the most qualified, best-educated hotelier who succeeds. It is the person with the drive and the passion who succeeds. You might have all the right qualifications and the years of experience under your belt but if you don't have what I call desire and people skills, you won't make it.

From me to you:

It is always you and nobody else who will make the difference between success and failure of your business. It is your vision, your drive, your work ethic, your strategy, and your sense of humour that sets your business apart from everybody else's.

Don't get discouraged by not knowing. Instead, start learning the trade.

Believe me, the first step to everything new is the hardest. As soon as you make your mental commitment to your new project and you take action, you will be amazed how the universe lends a helping hand and all the missing pieces start coming together.

Tom, the restaurant owner, referred me to his own coffee supplier, Marco. Marco not only sold coffee but everything else to go with it. For all I knew, I had to find a dark and medium roast Arabica blend for the coffee creations. My only stipulation was to stay away from the commonly known Dutch and Italian brands so widely used everywhere else. What Marco had to offer was exactly that. The coffee I chose was a dark roast with a slight tint of mocha. The taste was strong but not too strong. In short, his coffee was something I would drink myself with great pleasure and would come back for over and over again. The coffee flavour was not new to the market but it would be new to our guests. I liked the coffee taste so much I pre-ordered his coffee and sincerely hoped everybody else would share my taste.

To my greatest relief, this choice was very well-received by all our visitors. Everybody fell in love with it. The big coffee search was over before it even started. Without much time spent on comparing prices, I purchased the espresso maker, two grinders and a dishwasher – with big discounts – from Marco. (He was a lucky guy, don't you think?)

In order to finish the financial side of the business plan I needed an insurance quote for the future property. To speed things up I called our own agent, Inge. Our friendly chit-chat resulted in revealing my big plan. When Inge heard about the nature of the enterprise she gave me the telephone number of Rob. Rob was not only her nephew. He owned a bakery and bagel shops in Amsterdam.

Guess what he was selling? His business was making and selling US style cakes and bagels. I had to pinch myself to make sure I was hearing right. Without any hesitation, Inge handed me his telephone number. If his cakes were any good, this whole conversation must have been a set-up, arranged from a higher power. I called Rob straight away. We met up, I tasted his goods, and the rest is written in Bussum's history book.

My search for U.S-style goods had finished before it even started. And yes, his cakes were to-die-for, especially the cheesecake. All this took less travel time and fewer calorie intakes than expected. Rob's service was everything I was looking for. Better, his cheese-, carrot-, chocolate, and apple cakes were everything I was looking for. All products were baked in true American fashion and Rob's company also had a delivering system in place. I couldn't have dreamt this scenario any better.

From me to you:

Make your future business the best open secret in town. Talk about it; create a buzz. You will be amazed how many individuals are out there willing to help.

HELP. I DON'T HAVE A SUITABLE NAME FOR MY BUSINESS

So far the Strawberry story sounds pretty straight forward, doesn't it? A Google search here, a quick chat over there, one trip to Amsterdam for cake tasting and the bases of my enterprise were covered. If it were that easy, everybody would open up his or her own business.

Let's make it a bit more exciting...

To this day it still amazes me how fast and how easily everything fell into place – that is, until it was time to call the Chamber of Commerce to do a background check on the availability of my chosen name, RUBICON Coffee Lounge. Please note: This is very important. Your name has to be available from the Chamber of Commerce or other government agency in charge of business name registrations.

This was supposed to be a quick, routine check only. I expected a big, fat "Yes." The answer I received was, "No, sorry, the name Rubicon is unavailable."

The clerk found two businesses with the same name in our immediate neighbourhood. Both of them were unrelated to coffee but still, it was risky to use the name. Who wants to start their business life with a possible lawsuit? Couldn't I be any dumber? It turned out that "Rubicon" is one of the most widely used names for management companies in the Netherlands. The definition of the word is "to finish what you started", which is a perfect definition for any training, marketing or consultancy agency around.

Totally dumb-smacked and lost for words, I had to come up with a new name, and fast. Rubicon was my name, it was perfect for my purpose and I had never ever thought about an alternative. My venture needed a name since without a name there was no business. My brain went into overdrive mode.

Don't ask me why, but "Lemon Lounge" popped into my head. I found this quaint little place during my Internet searches for interior ideas. This coffee bar in New York looked fantastic on the inside. I liked the name, though not the word "lemon". Lemons leave a sour taste in your mouth. My coffee bar needed to be associated with sweet and warm. In the spur of the moment, I scribbled down all kinds of fruit I could remember while the helpful clerk from the registration office was on the line. The selection procedure was quite simple. I fired away the name of the fruit and Mr. Clerk gave his thumbs up or rejected it.

Mango Lounge? Not good. Mango is the name of a fashion house. They wouldn't be happy to be associated with coffee.

Pineapple Lounge? No, Sponge Bob and friends live in a pineapple.

Raspberry Lounge didn't have the right ring to it but it was available.

Apple Lounge? A perfect name for a farmers market but not for a coffee lounge in suburban Bussum.

Banana Lounge? Be honest. What are you thinking of right now? I will bet it has nothing to do with eating cheesecake in a smoke-free and child friendly environment.

Gooseberry, Blueberry, Peach, Orange Lounge? All these names were available but somehow they didn't have the right ring to any of them. Do you agree? A little bit further down the list we hit my favourite fruit of all time: The strawberry.

Actually, come to think of it, Strawberry Lounge sounded fabulous. And, the name was available. That's it. I thought. Strawberry Lounge will be the name of my first-ever, commercial enterprise, only seventeen years on the back burner in my head.

With the new name securely registered, Dominic and I did a survey among our friends. Everybody agreed that Strawberry Lounge was a fun name indeed. The name is catchy and the association with strawberries is even better. They look and taste good; they have a wonderful colour, are versatile in usage, and are healthy to eat.

Chander, the graphic designer, was the first person I called straight after deciding. "Change of plan," I said. "Please stop the press. We have to start all over again."

The whole process of creating a logo had to be repeated. At this stage we left the creative process in Chander's hands alone. We already spent lots of time together so I was convinced he knew what I wanted. There were more pressing matters to attend to, like retiring from the fitness world and finding the perfect location for Strawberry Lounge.

What a difference a name makes. All of a sudden the whole vision became crystal clear. I became more focused and couldn't wait to find a home for my business.

From me to you:

Do research for your name of choice early on; it can save you headaches.

I CAN'T FIND A LOCATION.

You think finding the right name in split seconds was exciting? Wait until you read this part of the story where I needed to find a vacant, suitable, inexpensive property.

Like every other city, Bussum operates with a town plan. The downtown shopping district is divided into *A* and *B* locations. An *A* location describes the main shopping street and its immediate side streets. Here you can find major retail outlets and the most pedestrian traffic. Any *A* location represents major exposure which equals high prices in rent. A *B* location refers to everything else. It means "off the beaten track", which in turn equals lower prices in rent.

When I realized how many coffees and cakes I had to sell just to pay rent on any *A* location I was highly motivated to seek out my ideal *B*. The centre of Bussum is not very big. Having Strawberry Lounge located off the beaten track was my perfect opportunity to make it a destination and not an accidental drop in.

If you want to start your own hospitality business you need a license to operate. Unlike different cities in different countries, a hospitality license here in Bussum is attached to the building, not to the business, i.e. there were only a handful of buildings that have been granted the status to operate. If you are familiar with this rule all you need to do is visit the planning department of the municipality and check out which buildings are eligible. This is a free, public service, available to anybody. If you were ignorant of this law – for example, you spent more time in fitness centers than inside the town hall – you strap your youngest son into his bike seat and start cycling around town.

Believe me when I say I circled our town several times, scribbling down every vacant shop, meeting with their representing agents. As soon as I mentioned the word hospitality, the red flag came up. "Sorry, this building doesn't have a license." I don't know how long it took me to finally figure out the name of the game.

I know what you are thinking. I had failed to do the proper groundwork – again. But as I told you, I was an aerobics instructor. What did I know about licensed buildings? Plus, lawmakers write and speak fluent municipality Dutch. This kind of Dutch literacy was so far above my third-grade level of understanding that I couldn't read it anyway. Ask me anything about re-registration and qualifications in the fitness world and you won't hear the end of it from me.

Anyway, it took me a few bike rides, a lot more conversations and lots more "no s" to finally figure out which direction the wind was coming from.

How does the saying go about insanity? Insanity is doing the same thing over and over again and expecting a different outcome.

Finally, I changed my approach. With a handful of addresses, I marched straight into the planning department. Sadly, the dreaded word kept on coming.

The search became annoying and frustrating, to say the least. After many more fruitless visits to the planning department I had to face the truth. There was not one licensed, spare shop to rent in all of Bussum.

If I wanted to proceed with my big plan I only had one option – the one I had never, ever considered – to buy an existing business and pay for the immensely high-priced goodwill. This option was way out of my league because most cafes and restaurants for sale had a price tag of Euro 100,000 ($140,000) attached to them.

I started having second thoughts about my project. It seemed much easier and less costly to open up a take-away coffee bar instead. The perfect location for a Strawberry Take-Away would be at the local train station. Travellers would leave their cups with my logo on the train and would carry the name all around the Netherlands. It seemed like a perfect alternative plan. Unfortunately, it was miles away from what I really wanted. "Christina, stay focused," I kept on telling myself. "Stay focused…"

It was hard. First of all, I hate rejections of all forms, shapes and words. I was worried about losing my momentum, excitement and enthusiasm. My search for a perfect home for Strawberry Lounge had hit rock bottom. On the bright side, I became very familiar with all the empty stores in Bussum, met lots of agents and became a familiar face at the planning department. Still, fact was fact. There wasn't one vacant shop in Bussum with a hospitality license attached to it. The licensed businesses for sale, on the other hand, had very high asking prices attached to their names. How high was my level of desperation? How badly did I want my dream to come true? How much was I willing to tweak my dream?

In order to pursue Option Two, I had to start visiting casinos or start buying lottery tickets. Both of them were neither practical nor tolerated by my own belief system. What else was there to do? Should I give up? Should I add another excuse to my already long list of existing ones? It is so easy to give up and say, "Oh well, I did my best, now there is nothing else for me to do or to try."

But like a rock climber holding on with the last ounce of strength, I pulled myself out of this dip and decided it wasn't time to quit yet. There was still some steam left. Desperation can be a resourceful companion at times. My head was spinning but what was the solution? I knew the municipality refused to hand out new licenses. But why wouldn't and couldn't the council make an exception? Instead of resigning and feeling sorry for myself I had to ask this question to the right person. What did I have to lose, apart from my own pride, and looking foolish?

IF NOBODY ELSE CAN, THE MAYOR CAN

The only person in power to help was the mayor himself. I needed to ask him to change the town plan on my behalf. With sweaty palms, I placed a call to his secretary. The secretary of our local mayor at that time, Dr. Milo Schoenmaker, listened to my heartfelt introduction and set up an appointment with the man himself. Poor Mr.Schoenmaker. Little did he know what he got himself into. With interest he listened to the idea of Bussum being in desperate need of a family-oriented, cozy coffee lounge. I made it clear I desperately needed his help to get the plan off the ground.

My question went something like this: "Mr. Schoenmaker, could you please hand out a hospitality license to a commercial property of my choice?" To this day I don't know if our mayor thought this was a serious request or if I played a trick on him. As a true professional he treated me with respect and explained in a serious manner the process necessary to help my cause. He actually liked my idea and welcomed my initiative. However, a mayor can only do so much. His hands are tied to rules and regulations like anybody else's.

To make the long, legislative story short and less boring, you need to know this information only: Nine months. It could take up to nine months to get my application through and (or most likely not) approved by the chamber members. This was my perfect excuse to throw in the towel.

No commercial property owner in his right mind would keep his shop on hold for nine long months. At this moment I couldn't think of another way forward. I was back at square one.

The outcome was disappointing but meeting our mayor made me feel good. At least I took action and didn't rely on luck, hope or prayers.

I CAN'T TAKE IT ANYMORE

I needed a new strategy. To get anything off the ground I had to buy an existing business. It was as simple as that. The "how-to" was still a big question but this was something to worry about later on. For now, I had to find a property, the perfect, most inexpensive, licensed property in a perfect *B* location. How hard could that be?

Over the course of my search one bistro in particular caught my eye: Le Pierrot. It was run down in condition, bad in reputation but in a perfect *B* location. The asking price was the lowest of all the available properties. It was 65,000 Euro ($84.500). Regardless of the pricetag I made Le Pierrot the first choice to pursue further. Its perfect *B* location was a five-minute walk from the main shopping street. You wouldn't necessarily visit the street if you weren't in need of a new haircut, new shoes or inexpensive clothes. The location didn't scare me – it was off the beaten track but it was perfect. At this location Strawberry Lounge could become the best-kept secret in town. It could become a destination and not an accidental stop because you happen to pass by.

The bistro had two terraces to call its own. Both terraces guaranteed sun from first thing in the morning till the early evening hours (that is, whenever the sun would be out). Another selling point is the adjacent underground parking garage. Arriving by car is the perfect alternative to the bike in case of a downpour. Le Pierrot was tucked in between a very trendy and a very busy street. It was ideal for everything I had in mind. Please check it out on www.strawberrylounge.nl.

The next big questions were, how much money could I buy it for and, how much work needed to be done on the inside?

My budget had a very limited amount set aside for any renovation or restoration work. The inside of Le Pierrot was one dark brown mess of heavy furniture, fluorescent light beams and flimsy curtains. In a classical sense, it was *The Tudors* meets *Star Wars*. It was clear to see the interior mastermind behind this classy mess has never watched any of the home furnishing or restaurant rescue shows.

If that wasn't bad enough, the open kitchen represented chaos. The serving space and the kitchen were divided by an old bar. Even a novice like me knows an open kitchen should represent spick and span equipment and working materials. Not in this one.

Shamelessly, this kitchen displayed the decay of its heart and soul. The fridges were held together by duck tape, the shelves were overflowing with cheap, dirty plates, pots and pans. Somewhere, lurking in the dark was a gas stove, several microwaves and an oven. The ceiling lights were on but for good measure and more appropriate lighting, the proprietor opted for additional spotlights. He chose the cheap clip-on variety. You are not going to believe what was missing from this kitschy kitchen – natural light and ventilation i.e. the kitchen didn't have a window.

Despite the poor display of hygiene, tidiness and co-ordination, the kitchen and serving area worked well together. Both had seen better days and were going downhill. The bistro presented itself in the worse possible light. One can imagine the reason for this sad state of affairs:

It was the current proprietor, an obese man, greasy from the hair on his head down to his apron and his dirty hands.

"The fish stinks from the head down," is a valid observation of how bad things trickle down from the owner to his business. In other words: Do you represent your business, or does the business represent you?

In the case of Le Pierrot, they went hand-in-hand. How was it possible and justified to ask so much money for this piece of garbage? It must have been something I had overlooked. For $84,000 I expected rows of customers lining up to fill his bistro. A cafe can be run down in appearance but still be popular among its clientele if, for example, the food is extremely good.

Once again, my son, Cruz, had the privilege of accompanying his mom on her mission. Instead of finding the perfect property, she needed to find out the secret behind $ 84,000.

Surprise, surprise. The few times we visited this eclectic shamble we were always the only visitors. Amazing personalities, wittiness, humour, or supreme customer service talents could make up for a lot of decay, but sadly, the greasy proprietor (Mr. Grease from now on) didn't display any of the above. We were served and politely ignored afterwards. After our lonesome, mother and child bonding experiences, the asking price seemed even more outrageous than before.

Please remember: 65,000 Euro wasn't the amount to buy part of the property. The sum was allocated to buy out the proprietor for the privilege to take over his greasy, filthy, rotten, non-existent business. Hoping, wishing and praying won't make it far in the world of business. There was only one way forward to make this place mine: Quickly Christina, find some money. Money talks or you have to walk.

Something had to be done about the price. The proper procedure to purchase a business in Holland is to get in touch with the representing agent to negotiate on the price. I sidestepped this rule by talking to the proprietor directly. For some unknown reason, Mr. Grease was adamant that his business was worth 65,000 Euro and not a penny less. If that was his final word, I had to double check with his representing agent. What can I tell you? The agent and Grease were in it together. He didn't budge on the price either. This ridiculous amount of money haunted me for days and weeks to come.

Dominic was appalled about the price and their non-negotiating attitude. He tried everything to convince me Le Pierrot wasn't the spot for me and to look further for something cheaper and different. Once again, I heard my perfect excuse. Dominic couldn't figure out why I was in a rush to open up my coffee business. He figured, "You waited this long, why can't you wait until something cheaper comes along?"

Why couldn't I? That's a good question. I said it earlier, there is never the perfect time to do something, the circumstances will never be right either. I needed to get on with it now. If not now, then when exactly would I?

Truth be told, there was no way I could ever get hold of this amount of money. I am naive but not naive and stupid at the same time, I thought, or am I? The dream was slipping away and there was nothing I could do.

A few weeks down the road we finally found out the real reason behind the asking price: Mr. Grease was up to his neck in debts – months and months of unpaid rent were in his name. The 65,000 Euro were his lifeline. Now we knew why he was holding on. He was holding out until someone would throw him a life raft. Should I be the one? Let's find out what the owner of the building had to say about his client, I thought.

Under normal circumstances the landlord has nothing to do with the purchase of an existing business. His only responsibility is to check the credibility of the new owner before he lets him sign the new lease agreement. I had a goal to chase and the intention to make it happen. Goals don't fall under the category "normal circumstances". I made the call. To protect the real identity of my ex-landlord, I will call him William. The gentleman still operates in the area and to call him William is much better than my chosen alternative, "Mr. Greed".

William is in the real estate business to make money, not to help out, and not to make friends. Thanks to him, this forty-year-old, very nice mother of three received her first hard-core lesson in business: It is all about cold, hard cash. Stupid me, I thought it was more about building and nurturing relationships. Yes, you are right, I entered the business world like a love struck teenager.

William wanted money too. He gladly waved the 65,000 Euro but still wanted an undisclosed amount from me to take over Mr. Grease's business. In other words, he wanted me to pay off his debts. In return I would get what I wanted and needed so badly, a licensed business.

I was such a bad poker player. William took one look into my eyes and knew I was his. All he needed to do was drum his message in over and over again. For much less than the asking price the bistro could be mine. He certainly was a persistent man, since he kept on drumming. Like a broody, desperate woman I said yes. Looking back, I must have been maddening crazy or crazily mad.

With my signature on the rental contract I bought myself a five-year time frame within to start and build Strawberry Lounge (standard agreement in Dutch hospitality law). Furthermore, I received fifty square meters floor space worth of useless stuff, fifty square meters full of garbage in the basement, a period of twenty-three rent-free days and the magic license. During the hormonal turmoil of signing my "life away for the next five years" I sincerely forgot about the money I had to pay to William. I didn't have enough. All my previous business calculations were based on renting and furnishing a business, nothing else.

Of course, I had funds available. The money available had to buy furniture, coffee equipment and everything else that makes a business a business. Mentally, I ran through the options available to get hold of the needed cash. Going to a bank was the easiest solution. Before a bank even considers giving me money I needed a security of some sort. Would Dominic be willing to be my guarantor? And, if a bank were willing to lend me money, they would charge steep interest rates for their service. All in all, banks can be an option but they are expensive. Option two and three were either to ask my parents or one of my aunts in Germany for a private loan. One person I didn't want to ask was Dominic For me it was a matter of personal pride. I wanted to show him that I could do it all by myself.

From me to you:

Do not get emotionally attached to a location, a property or any other deal whatsoever. If you do, let someone else do the talking and negotiation for you. Be willing to walk away. There will be new, cheaper places coming up, eventually. If you run away you need to promise yourself and me to stay focused though. You need to keep on searching.

In hindsight, this was the most valuable lesson I have learned during my adventure. This is a tough one – how is it possible to walk away from something you really, really wanted. It is easier said than done. Picture a woman on the brink of a hormonal breakdown. Ask your husband or mine, "Is it impossible to reason with an unreasonable person?" I bet he will say no.

Where was Dominic, my wonderful knight in shining armour? Why didn't he help me during the negotiating period? I told you, I didn't let him. Another reason was, he knew better. We have known each other for a long time. The husband just has to know when to back off. The flip side of completing the deal all by myself was the near end of our marriage (Just kidding. Dominic threatened divorce with a twinkle in his eyes. We are still happily married to this day.) He had every right to feel that way but deep down, I hoped he would be proud of me, too. His mad wife showed perseverance and succeeded.

It was one of my happiest moments when I signed the rental contract. Finally, after a gestation period of nearly seventeen years, baby number four was ready to be born. I was ready to embark on my second biggest adventure yet. In case you are interested in knowing what the first one is, it is raising our boys.

I DON'T HAVE ANY (ENOUGH) MONEY

We all need money to do whatever it is we want to do in life. Regardless of the kind of business you want to start, it will cost you.

My parents set up a savings account for both my brother and me back in Germany. Over the years the account accumulated approximately 25,000 Euro ($32,500) ready to be spent as a down payment for an apartment or to furnish my first house. This account was earmarked for fixtures and fittings for The Strawberry Lounge. Very soon, I had to check with my parents if they could lend me money for my purchase. Before I could even get to the phone, a rescue angel handed over a cheque with the words: "Go for it, girl. I believe in you. I know you can do it."

I was shocked beyond words and tears came streaming down my face. The person who handed over the cheque was Dominic. I knew he loved me but I never knew he trusted me with such an enterprise. To me, this cheque meant more than any, "I love you". In my eyes his money represented love in combination with trust and true belief in my enterprise and me. What a great feeling that was. My own husband invested in my teenage dream.

His trust and belief in Strawberry Lounge let me grow wings. I vowed not to disappoint him. Why do you think Dominic gave me the money? Most probably, he had enough of my whining and non-stop speculations about things in the far future. He wanted his quiet, peace and sanity back. He figured money could buy all three things. Furthermore, it was a perfect opportunity to find out if he married a hot air balloon or a woman of substance. Let his wife prove to him and the rest of the world what she was really made of.

This unexpected loan left me with my savings free to use for its original purpose. Best of all, I didn't need a bank loan. I'd rather pay my husband back with a lower interest rate than a bank with their steep rates. All I needed was a bank guarantee for the landlord and the show was on the road.

Still in the dark about how much money a coffee lounge would actually generate, I asked the bank for an overdraft facility to keep me afloat during my first year in business. After the bank received my money for the rent guarantee they granted me an overdraft for 2,000 Euro.

If you need money, what are your options?

Personally, I recommend getting as much financing done through you or through private sources. If your idea is in the far future, start saving now. Banks, in general, prefer giving money to individuals who can show own capital, who have a guarantee of value (e.g. a house, an apartment or property) or at least a guarantor who vouches for them.

We later found out Dutch banks don't like lending money to hospitality start-ups. Hospitality businesses in general are considered "risky" businesses because nobody knows for sure what makes a restaurant, bar or cafe successful. And nobody can pinpoint why guests prefer one spot over the other, especially bankers.

I know of two cafes on a family beach in Holland. They are fifty meters (150 yards) apart from each other. Both look alike, both offer a similar menu, they play the same music, the waitresses in both huts look cool and trendy. The only difference is: One is packed and the other is not. And nobody knows why.

Apart from the well-known high street banks, there are banks around who specialize in helping start-ups or who specialize in supporting certain business sectors. You will find this information on Google.

Another source for a private loan would be family members or good acquaintances. One word of caution, friends and money don't mix well together. I could tell you a story or two about that.

To generate some cash you could make sacrifices on a personal level, e.g. you could sell your car (this only works if your alternative transportation will be cheaper than an automobile). Another idea is to rent out part of your apartment or to rent out a room in your house. I know this option sucks if you like your privacy. Some individuals even go as far as re-mortgaging their house in order to finance their business idea.

Apart from calculating the start-up and running costs of your enterprise, you also need to know exactly how high your monthly personal costs will be. It may turn out you have to make some more personal sacrifices in order to get your idea off the ground, e.g. fewer trips to your favourite restaurant, cheaper holidays or less expensive clothes, to name just a few.

Have you heard of angel investors? These are men and women who will invest in your business idea in return for a chunk of your enterprise – if they believe in the concept and are convinced your calculations add up. (Think of the TV show *Dragons Den*). Some angel investors are attached to certain business sectors only, e.g. information technology or property. You can find out about these angels in business periodicals, business publications or on Google.

Unfortunately, not everybody has their own investor sleeping right next to them. I know I was very lucky. However, as you read, I had my alternatives lined up.

From me to you:

We all need money to live. Some of us believe we need more than others. In so many cases it is not the case of not having or earning enough, it is how we choose to spend it. Making personal sacrifices is the biggest hurdle for most.

STAYING DEBT FREE

To make the most of my limited funds I needed a plan to stay out of debt. One thing was for sure – I couldn't skimp on equipment. A good chunk of the money went towards the purchase of the best espresso maker and coffee bean grinders the market had to offer. To refurbish my enterprise I didn't look any further than the biggest second-hand store in our area. I was on a mission to purchase original, inexpensive furniture for the whole shop. To our Dutch friends it sounded like business suicide. Why? Bussum is part of t'Gooi, one of the most affluent areas in Holland.

The owners of restaurants, shops and cafés charge high prices for everything they offer. They figured, "We might as well. The people who live here have to have a big income. If they can afford to buy a house in t'Gooi they can afford to pay premium prices for food and services." To complete the circle, most residents expect state-of-the-art furniture, fabulous crockery, and small portions.

I wasn't too worried about my plan of execution but everybody else was. Deep down, I knew the plan would work. Because, **it is not what you sell but how you sell it.**

I strongly believe the product you serve is so much more important than the chair you sit in. Who cares if the couch costs $1000.00 or $10.00, as long as it is comfortable and clean? Still, the proof is in the pudding and I had to put the theory to the test. Our guests had to decide for themselves.

All in all, it was exciting, challenging, and an adventure to have a limited budget to play with. How easy would it be to have a big sum available to purchase anything and everything the heart desires? Anyone can do that. Having lots of money available may let you forget about being creative.

Only heaven knows how many blissful hours I spent in the thrift store. Every single item needed to create the cozy, "just like home" feel came from there. The only standardized items I bought were coffee cups and glasses because every cup of coffee sold, small or large, had to be the same size.

I couldn't expect everybody to sit low and lounge while eating their bagel or cake; therefore we bought a few standard size kitchen tables from IKEA. My four low-sitting couches came from the same shop. We stained the kitchen tables and dyed the couch covers to give them a very individualistic look.

From me to you:

If you are in the process of starting your first-ever business then take this as your perfect opportunity to follow your heart. Create what you really wanted all along - and stay away from well-wishers who want to dictate what, in their opinion, is right or wrong.

If you have limited funds available remember, a layer of paint and tie-dye can make all the difference in the world to the appearance of your walls or furniture. With more creativity than money you can achieve a very individualistic look.

SHOULDN'T I GET A PARTNER?

Wouldn't it be so much easier to have a business partner to share the workload? To bounce ideas off? To share the financial risk? Have I ever thought about a partnership with somebody else?

Never. I like to play on a team, however, only if the team is as good or as bad as I am do I feel comfortable in my role as team member. I don't like pulling the weight, nor do I like being the burden. The idea of my beach café had been in my head for so long and my vision was so clear. It would have been very hard to share this feeling with someone else.

Without a doubt, it is risky to start a business. Are you thinking about getting a partner? Here are some pointers to consider:

Are you willing to risk a financial meltdown? Are you willing to put your family life on hold? Can you give up leisure time for a certain period of time in your life? Are you ready to face consequences for your actions?

Starting up a business comes in a package full of surprises, frustration, headaches, fun and tears. If this sounds daunting, consider finding a partner to share the emotional roller coaster.

I was willing to give up on any of the above plus my life's savings. I didn't want or needed a partner. All of a sudden our acquaintances, friends and even strangers told me what an impact running my own shop would have on my family life. I didn't want to know. My ears were conveniently shut during these conversations.

Thank God, I didn't know what to expect when I entered the business world. I had no idea how the journey would end and I had no idea about right and wrongs in the hospitality business. If you bask in the warm glow of ignorance you have nothing to worry about.

Believe me, quite often it is much better to know too little than it is to know too much about your subject matter. The more you know, the more you are worried about things. You worry about procedures and consequences. On the contrary, you cannot be afraid of something you don't even know exists. Based on this logic, I was ready to take on motherpreneurship with all its highs and lows. In return, any rewards and possible glory would all be mine.

Having a partner was not an option. I needed help instead.

My first treasured employee was Marcello. He was one of these bright young men you find working behind the coffee counter of a gym. Marcello was ready for a change in scenery and more than willing to help me during the set-up and starting phase. Another Godsend was my friend Ulrica, who offered to work with me on a part-time basis. Her involvement would give me time off to pick up the boys from school and to do the necessary housekeeping at home. I liked, trusted and treasured them both and was so excited to start Strawberry Lounge with them.

THIS IS TOO MUCH WORK

The clock was ticking. We had twenty-three days before the first rent payment was due. My persistence and stubbornness bought fifty square meters filled from top to bottom with filth. On receiving word of the take-over, Mr. Grease just left. He left his brasserie without taking anything with him. His apron was still hanging on the hook when I arrived the next day. His fridges and freezers were full; the dirty dishes were still in the dishwasher.

If you are on a tight budget you might roll up your sleeves and get on with the job at hand. If you have a few nice friends invite them along for a thorough whirlwind cleaning party.

The only item I spent money on was a big skip I rented for all the useless rubbish I purchased.

Time was ticking away; we had to prioritize what to do first. We needed to get the upstairs done as soon as possible. The downstairs was filled with rubble, rubbish, food items, freezers, refrigerators, boxes filled with jars, plastic bags, menu cards, receipts, cook books, pots, pans, flower pots, Christmas decorations – you name it. Anything and everything could be found in one of the boxes in the basement.

Our boys loved all this chaos. Too many times they reappeared from the cellar with newfound treasures in their tiny hands.

The freezers and fridges in the basement were full. Due to a very narrow staircase we couldn't get them out. To this day I still wonder how these massive boxes appeared in the cellar. Have you ever smelled a whole freezer or fridge full of old, rotten fish and meat? Yes it happens, even in a freezer. All you need to do is set the temperature on its lowest setting. It is the worst stink imaginable. I had to put a bandana in front of my mouth to stop me from throwing up. Bags full of filthy, rotten veggies, casseroles, fish and steaks ended up in the garbage container.

The kitchen upstairs had shelves overflowing with crockery, pots and pans. Secretly, I hoped Dominic's money bought at least some pots or crockery. Far from it. On closer inspection, we discovered most of the pots still contained leftover gravy from a while back. For good measure we dumped the whole kitchen inventory into the skip. It was a miracle Le Pierrot was still open during its last months of operation. Isn't this a good example of Murphy's Law? The health inspector always shows up when you least expect him but never when he should be expected.

The most treasured find we made was a hidden, blocked window in the kitchen. With much care we cut out the wood and voila, we created the light and ventilation so badly needed. For the stuffy furniture, I contacted a removal company who specialized in restaurant inventory. They picked up everything at no cost and even paid me for the stuff.

All these activities needed to be done during school hours or in the evening. My biggest help was the fabulous Dominic. We took turns looking after the boys in the evening or hired a baby sitter to do the work together. We even spent our anniversary on the demolition site.

Between destroying the old bar we drank champagne and dreamt about our future in the hospitality industry together. Actually, I need to rephrase this. I was daydreaming about my glorious future in the hospitality industry whereas he had nightmares about his future as houseman.

MARKETING? I HAVE NO CLUE ABOUT MARKETING. HOW CAN I GET FREE PUBLICITY?

Queen's Day, April 30th.

You have your business set up, your location is nearly presentable and you are looking for a cheap, easy way to promote your business. One of the cheapest ways is to look through your city's events calendar and take part in any event your community offers. Strawberry Lounge had the perfect opportunity to shine as a newbie during Holland's annual Queen's Day celebration. (From 2014 onwards it will be King's Day.)

Queen's Day is the biggest, most crazy public holiday in the Dutch calendar. It is a nationwide alfresco party celebrated in honour of Queen Beatrix – and by nature of the day it is a fun holiday.

The organizers offer live music, street vendors, flea markets, children activities and street performers. Sixteen million people are out and about enjoying themselves. Publicity and exposure are everything on this day. It is the biggest moneymaking day of the year for any shop owner, if you are willing to take part. Nothing compares to this day. Believe me, I've experienced it six times in a row. It is madness; it is scary and somewhat magical. You will run your socks off; you will have long rows of visitors lining up in front of your shop. You will be on the brink of going crazy, you won't know what to do first, your head will be spinning and you can't imagine you will be able to cope with the never ending influx of people walking into your store. But at the end of the day, when the finger pushes "Total" on the cash register, you will sigh and be in heaven.

The amount of money you make during Queen's Day alone makes up for a few slow weeks. Obviously, I know this now but I didn't know it when I started. As a family we experienced a few Queen's Days prior to my business adventure; I knew how crazy busy this whole day is.

In other words, I couldn't let this opportunity slip away. Strawberry Lounge had to be open on Queen's Day - at any cost.

BUT, I AM NOT READY YET. I WILL EMBARRASS MYSELF

An event like this is the perfect opportunity for your business to shine. And you are coming up with an excuse? Your business isn't presentable yet? What is missing exactly? How severe are these unfinished items? Is there a way you could compensate for them?

Strawberry Lounge (S.L.) was far from being ready or even perfect. Half the population of Bussum would walk pass the lounge – what better day was there to introduce the *new flavour in town*? The idea of being half-finished but fully open to the public was unconceivable to most of our Dutch acquaintances. They argued the first impression is the most important one for any business. They tried to convince me to make S.L. 100% presentable or shy away from being open.

"Are these people mad?" I thought. "What is a little unfinished business in exchange for half of Bussum to get to know us?" I was beginning to think just like a 'red' entrepreneur.

One of the most visible unfinished items of the lounge was the outside. Twenty-three days didn't buy us enough time to paint the facade. Marcello came up with a brilliant idea: We bought a few white bed sheets and red spray paint. In big, bright letters he wrote: "Strawberry Lounge – SPECIAL PREVIEW" on them.

It was a 'cover–up exposure', if you know what I mean. We hung these beauties along the scrappy awnings for everybody to see.

During my property and location search I recruited a Polish building company to design my bar and counters for the shop. The company would spring into action as soon as a suitable location was found. When this happened the workmen took the measurements. I decided on the kind of wood I liked most and we parted with the promise to meet again not later than April 29th to put the customized items into place. Apart from frantic cleaning, painting, repairing or fixing nothing noteworthy happened until this day.

True to the theme and chosen name one of our friends came up with the perfect colour scheme; strawberry red for the walls, coffee brown for the trim and cream white for everything else in between. Thanks to Chander we also had a logo (check it out: www.strawberrylounge.nl).

By April 29th the lounge was painted in these strawberry colours exactly. We didn't have any pictures hanging on the walls yet, however, the washrooms were painted, all the furniture was in place, the CD player was installed and I bought enough mix and match crockery for our goodies.

Deciding on how much I had to order was the hardest thing. How would I know how much we could sell? Sometimes it is hard being a first-timer to the business world. All I could do was place the order, hope for the best and "sell my heart out".

You just read about our crappy-looking awning and how we dealt with it. If you think this is kind of embarrassing, read on for the next unfinished item on the list.

We didn't have an espresso maker. Yes, you read this right. I would open up a coffee shop without an espresso maker. How did that happen? The professional semi-automatic espresso machine I purchased was wide, bulky and very heavy. This kind of machine requires a sturdy workbench to be placed upon and electricity.

Our electricity was available but we had no clue when our handmade worktops and bar would arrive on the 29th. As CEO, I decided not to have Marco, the coffee man, around in case he might waste his day waiting around. I knew about this fact far in advance. Instead of having freshly made coffee on offer we printed vouchers as a substitute. The voucher read: Receive a latte, cappuccino or black coffee for free with any cake purchase during our Grand Opening on Sat. May 6th.

During April 29th a few friends, Dominic and I worked frantically to get everything sorted for the following day. All day long we waited for the Polish workforce but no craftsmen came into sight. By evening we were still waiting and butterflies started to fly inside my tummy. Oh, how these insects made me nervous.

I knew I could get away without serving coffee but I knew I couldn't get away without a bar or workbench to prepare or serve from. All of us kept our fingers crossed. We wished, hoped and prayed for the best. Our combined effort was answered. In the middle of the night, at 11:45 PM to be precise, a fully loaded work truck stopped in front of Strawberry Lounge. The men made good on their promise and the missing, customized furniture was installed.

By the time the guys finished it was 2:30 in the morning. We had fewer than five hours until the unofficial opening. Deep down, my sub-consciousness was nagging me that something else was missing. What was it? It was annoying and frustrating not knowing what was missing. Suddenly, the penny dropped.

Are you ready for yet another unfinished item?

It was the kitchen faucet. Yes, you heard right. It was the faucet.

How on earth did I forget to buy a kitchen faucet? If that wasn't bad enough, where could we find one in the middle of the night? We definitely didn't have a spare one lying around at home, nor did anybody else have one. Let's recap the situation: It was 2:30 a.m., and in four and a half hours I would face the biggest day of my business life. I was about to open a family-friendly coffee lounge with no coffee to sell and no running water to wash our hands with or to boil water for tea.

Could this get any worse? The butterflies came back, this time with a vengeance. Panic set in, I became all sweaty and edgy. The only water sources available were the two washrooms. Holy Moly, this was one of those moments in life when you had to bite the bullet. "It just is what it is and there is no way around it." There would be no faucet during our Queen's Day Preview.

The mind works in mysterious ways, even during early morning hours. Our combined brains came up with the following solution: Dominic had to fill up jerry cans at our house and bring them to the Strawberry on his bicycle. That was the safest bet because we didn't know if our new neighbours would be home. Fortunately my wonderful husband was happy enough to play rescue angel and cycle back and forth.

From me to you:

Think differently.

No faucet? Become creative and think out of the box. There is always a solution for everything.

I can't give you specific solutions for your dilemmas, as I don't know what they are. Please feel free to drop me a line and I am more than happy to help (christinawaschko@gmail.com).

QUEEN'S DAY

Queen's Day starts at the crack of dawn with vendors putting up stalls in one part of town. At another part of town a huge flea market is set up. Sellers and buyers are up early to either find a prime spot to spread out their goods or to find and negotiate the best deals.

And then there is the third group, the hospitality proprietors who make sure their venue is ready to feed the early, cold and hungry crowd. From today onwards I would be part of the third group. You might not win a beauty contest after two and half hours of restless tossing and turning in your bed; however, the adrenaline pumping through your veins can make up for more than just lack of sleep.

I was psyched. I was so nervous, I nearly peed my pants. This was my day. Today was the unofficial birth of baby number four. I couldn't wait. It was 6:30 a.m. and the goal was to take Bussum by storm.

Marcello and two other friends agreed to help me on my first trial run for the Strawberry business. I opened the doors on a rainy, cold Queen's Day, April 30th 2006.

The light drizzle was a mixed blessing because our first, early visitors were only worried about finding shelter, a cup of hot tea, cookies or warm bagels. Any requests for coffee were shrugged off with a fun comment. Instead, we handed over our coffee voucher and convinced the coffee lover a hot chocolate or hot tea is the perfect substitute for the java drink. Where we convincing enough? We sure were. As soon as we ran out of hot chocolate the sun come out. She couldn't have timed it any better. Now we had the opportunity to sell our cold coffee shakes or fruit shakes to the thirsty masses. Our terraces were busy and our visitors were enjoying themselves. I was walking on clouds.

To cut a long story short, Queen's Day was a roaring success. We got away with murder, with no running water from the tap or an espresso machine to make coffee. A happy, prosperous day doesn't need any explanation or excuses. I like to name the factors anyway which helped to create this wonderful success.

Parts of it can be blamed on the day itself. People are much friendlier, more helpful and easier to forgive on Queen's Day. By the end of the afternoon most Queen's Day visitors are slightly tipsy anyway, so they couldn't care less if you had coffee or not. We sold our goods with unprecedented enthusiasm, big smiles, and we offered a freebie. Don't we all love a voucher for something free?

All our brownies, bagels and cakes were sold by the end of the day. Our friend, Richard, sold the last few remaining chocolate chip cookies. He put them on a tray and sold them to the last passers-by in the street.

What an exceptional, exciting day it was. It was magic to see so many faces walking through the door. Everybody had a friendly word for us, and our goodies were much appreciated, praised and complimented. Remember, Strawberry Lounge wasn't perfect but it received all the free publicity I anticipated.

After this very successful day, a good night rest, and a day off for the family, we had to roll up our sleeves again – this time to make Strawberry Lounge as perfect and presentable as possible.

From me to you:

When presented with this once in a year opportunity, timed exactly one week before the grand opening, when everybody around you advised you not to do it, would you have done the same? What would you have done instead?

THE FINAL COUNTDOWN - HELP, ONLY 6 MORE DAYS.

We had six full days to get Strawberry Lounge into ship-shape condition for the Grand Opening the following Saturday, the sixth of May. Marco delivered my espresso machine first thing on Monday morning. He set it up and gave us a crash course on how to use it, the proper cleaning procedure, how to regulate and change the density of the coffee powder in the grinders and most of all, how to make the most amazing froth ever.

I had to learn everything. As soon as he started on the mechanical part, it became like Chinese to me. I opted to cheat and asked for the direct line to one of his mechanics. In case of emergency he could talk me through the necessary steps of first aid for an espresso machine. I am not saying his equipment would break down but I needed to have a backup plan in case something went wrong. It is never the equipment by itself breaking down; it is always humans who push the wrong buttons or twist a knob too tightly. Calling him became a very useful, tried and tested routine many times over. I highly recommend this procedure, especially if you are working with staff that has no clue about mechanics.

That same day, I purchased the faucet and the kitchen was ready for action. One of my buddies from school painted the logo on the tiles in the kitchen (www.strawberrylounge.nl). Four young painters transformed the outside of old Le Pierrot into a coffee brown gateway into Strawberry heaven. The bed sheets were replaced with real letters and our logo. Marcello, Ulrica and I practiced our coffee making skills. We decided which toppings to use for the bagels; we practiced on the till and figured out a serving system.

We hung up posters announcing the Grand Opening at various shops, the library and our school. The local newspaper received an ad from me to announce the arrival of the *new flavour.* More than anything else, I relied on our friends to spread the word and their promises to join us for the opening.

The big day approached too fast and too soon. But unlike six days before, this time Strawberry Lounge was ready. Everything was perfect and in working order. The fridges were stocked, the cakes were out on display and our first, basic bagel menu was designed and ready to be put to the test.

THE GRAND OPENING
THIS IS IT, NO MORE EXCUSES.

The Weather Goddess ordered sunshine for Saturday. She knew full well what a special day it would be for my family and me. Somewhat naïve, I took the sun as a sign for future prosperity of my coffee shop. My butterflies were back but this time they were dancing in anticipation, excitement and pride. Once again, I couldn't wait to get going. Everything was set up and prepared by 10 a.m. Marcello and Ulrica showed up, which instantly calmed me down. All three of us were excited, ready for what the day might bring. All we needed to do was wait. In silence all three of us pleaded: "Please, please, please dear friends, acquaintances and residents of Bussum, show up. We have something new and exciting for you."

I believe in self-affirmation and visualization. It was either that or the wonderful, bright sunny Saturday morning that lured Bussumers outside, straight onto our two terraces.

We welcomed our friends and families. Acquaintances from all walks of life came by to offer their congratulations. Our new neighbours wished us well and the curious passersby were pleased to find something new in Bussum. Even my parents decided to take the five-hour trip from

Kiel to Bussum to surprise me, to celebrate with us and to lend a hand if we needed one. Baker Rob, restaurant owner Tom, our mayor and the Canadian boys all made an appearance to check out what I had created. Mind you, they had heard me talking about it for long enough.

Along with our first guests, the first vouchers reappeared. Our cakes sold like hot cakes, our complimentary coffees received fullest praise. At first, the use of fresh milk startled our visitors but after a few sips, they enjoyed the new taste experience. We were busy all right, but not too crazy that we couldn't enjoy ourselves.

Thank God, no major mishaps happened, no major dramas, no spillages, no cold or too hot coffees were served. I believe the only downer of the whole day was the waiting time for cappuccino and macchiato our guests ordered. We hadn't acquired the skill set of experienced baristas yet. Our guests had to wait a bit but didn't seem to mind. All in all, we experienced another fantastic day.

Our opening day made enough money to cover all the expenses with enough money over to raise my confidence. Surely that must be another good omen.

All of Sunday was filled with the glorious feeling of success. For the following Monday I envisioned rows of happy people lining up to enjoy my newcomer to town.

During the first few months of "Operation Strawberry Lounge", we were closed on Sundays. We started our week on Monday at 1 p.m. Most shops in Bussum open their doors at the same time so as a newcomer to the business world I figured I should follow suit.

DAILY GRIND
ONE BIG EMBARRASSMENT
HOW CAN I GET CUSTOMERS?

Our first official Monday was soon to be our official day off. I am not kidding. We opened our doors at 1 p.m. just like the rest of our business community and it proved to be a lonely Monday for Marcello. It was so quiet all afternoon that he had a real challenge to keep himself busy for the next four hours. All he sold were a few coffees and few muffins. What an embarrassment and disappointment it was. I took it personal – literally. I honestly believed all of Bussum was waiting to queue up to get a glimpse of the wonderful, new Strawberry Lounge. Fortunately, as the week progressed, so did business.

Ulrica, Marcello and I worked in shifts, either alone or as a team. It was a blessing in disguise that the lounge wasn't busy yet. We had to learn so many different, new things on the go while we were doing the job. For example, Rob's baking instructions didn't work for my kind of oven. We baked and wasted lots of bagels and muffins until the perfect temperature was found. We had to figure out defrosting times for the various cakes. We experimented with different cheeses to find the perfect bagel-cheese melting ratio without making the bagel too hard to serve.

Looking back I have to give our newfound guests and future friends big credit for their patience. Our early regulars experienced many irregularities and most of them took it with grins on their faces. As I just mentioned, I tried and tested various cheeses for our bagels, and so did our guests. Our scrambled eggs arrived on their plates either too salty or not seasoned at all. For the sake of keeping slicing interesting, our tomato slices came in all different sizes and thickness levels. And who said that your pieces of cake needed to be all the same size? Where is it written that all flavoured coffees needed exactly the same number of syrup shots?

Are you shaking your head in disbelief? Come on, be honest, you just did. You also wanted to ask me this question: "Why didn't you figure all these things out before you opened your door for business?"

Honestly, I don't have an answer to this question. All in all, I was still pretty clueless about everything. I was a rookie in the best sense of the word. I was a fitness instructor turned motherpreneur with more guts than knowledge. I had more enthusiasm than money; I had a dream and no inkling.

The three of us as a team were on a learning curve. Most of our early guests seemed to feel, understand and appreciate our efforts to look professional. Deep down they applauded our efforts and tried to keep the smirks off their faces when yet another piece of cake was smaller than the previous one and their coffee was a bit sweeter than the last one they ordered.

From me to you:

There is nothing wrong with learning the job while doing the job. Only practice makes perfect. Just get on with doing what you do and do the best job you can do.

That's what the three of us did, and one day we became fabulous. I was never perfect. I became fluent, highly efficient, very skilled but never, ever perfect. I was good. I became a kick ass barista but was never the perfect one. The one thing I always have been: I was the best hostess you could find in Bussum.

Our first week was doubly exciting for the fact that I had to figure out how to fit my children into my new life as motherpreneur. Up 'til now it was fun – rehearsal time – but with our official opening it became very serious. I had signed a five-year lease contract.

I had to figure out at what time I had to leave home to drop the kids off at school. My morning routine for home had to become very regimented. I didn't have time for errors, forgotten homework, last minute face painting, or finding empty toilet paper rolls for an arts project.

For Strawberry Lounge I needed to design a shopping system, a shopping route, a delivering system for Rob's cakes and bagels, a laundry system and a cleaning routine. I bought the newspaper every day, plus glossy magazines, which was horrendously expensive (let's not forget time consuming) in the long run. With time and research I figured out it was much cheaper to subscribe to the newspaper and magazines and have them delivered on a daily or monthly basis.

From day one onwards it was "project labour of love" for me. I welcomed Strawberry Lounge into our lives like I would a new baby. This was my business baby now and I was determined to make a walking, talking adult out of it.

I HAVE NO CLUE HOW TO BUILD A BUSINESS

As I wrote earlier, Strawberry Lounge wasn't busy at the start. Therefore, we had the time to chat with every single one of our new guests. By the time they left us we knew their name, the name of their dog, their children's names and the size of their shoes.

When you are selling your services to the crowd you must know about the power of relationships. Relationship is the magic word that makes your business stay around for a long, long time. Without your paying visitors you wouldn't have a business, so build relationships with your most favoured guests. If you don't like to chat, if you don't like to listen and chat some more, you are in the wrong business.

And yes, I love to chat, as do Ulrica and Marcello. Our efforts started to pay off. During the coming weeks we saw our first familiar faces. Our familiar faces always brought somebody new along for us to meet and to spoil. We were on the right track and our Strawberry family started to grow.

What makes a business thrive? How does it make money? The obvious rule is to keep costs down so you can maximize your profit. Further along the line every enterprise needs referrals and repeat business.

The surest way to get your guests coming back is to offer a fantastic product coupled with an affordable price. I wanted to sell volume due to a somewhat lower price structure and, hopefully, have the lounge busy most of the time.

During the first few months we welcomed the good, the bad and the ugly. Apart from the few really nice visitors who stayed loyal to us for years I had the snobs who were appalled by my slightly lower prices. In no uncertain terms they told me, "The prices are too low. You can't be serving good quality."

We had the winos that used to come to the former bistro sitting and staring at their bottle of beer, looking scrappy, talking rubbish. Winos were the totally wrong crowd for my coffee lounge. They were screaming *bad image*. How could I get rid of them? Is it appropriate to say, "Please leave, you are not welcome here?" No, that isn't me. As long as they paid and didn't disturb our harmonious lounge business I behaved like the perfect hostess and let them stay. Thankfully, after a short while our winos didn't feel at home anymore. It must have been the constant smell of coffee in the air that didn't mix well with beer.

Our perfect guests were open-minded and well travelled. They experienced the coffee drinking culture in other parts of the world and appreciated the flair of Starbucks®-like experience in small town Bussum. Our biggest fans were the newbies to Bussum who had moved from Amsterdam or any other big city. We reminded them of their previous city life and everybody else of their holidays somewhere in Florida. The lounge brought something cosmopolitan to Bussum. Was this due to my ongoing conversations in Dinglish (English/Dutch/German all in one sentence)? If I couldn't live my dream on a Caribbean island at least I could pretend to behave as if I was. I had to draw the line at wearing a bikini top though.

I CAN'T HOLD OUT ANY LONGER, EVERYBODY IS GIVING ME SHIT.

My business plan mentioned parents and children as preferred target group. During the start-up phase I got cold feet and I got worried. How much money would parents be willing to spend with and on their children? Could I survive with only serving parents? To be on the safe side I wanted to keep "the club" open and accessible to as many individuals as possible. More visitors meant more money... or not? At this early stage in my new career I was still a business virgin and unfamiliar with the concept of niche marketing.

With this in mind I welcomed everybody into the lounge and wanted to please them all.

During the next few weeks it became apparent we couldn't please everybody. Lots of people showed up, complained, and left again. No kidding, it is hard to accommodate personal preferences from so many people from different walks of life. You probably knew that. To me this was quite a revelation.

Let me share with you what people complained about:

"I am not allowed to smoke in here?" (In 2006, you were still allowed to smoke in most hospitality facilities. Strawberry Lounge was non-smoking from Day One onwards.

"You don't offer enough choices on the menu." (www.strawberrylounge.nl, click on liquids.)

"Your coffee tastes different. I like the one from the other place better."

"Your opening times, newspaper on offer and music sucks."

"You are not expensive enough, how can this be good quality."

"Yuckie, cheesecake and carrot cake."

Welcome to The Netherlands, the land of legalized marijuana and open, direct speech. Citizens from around the world have different ways of expressing their complaints.

For example, the English are *uber*-polite and offer an excuse with their complaint. The Germans shout, yell and shout, the American sugar coats, Canadians are friendly, concise and informative with their complaint, the Aussies take the mickey and leave. The Dutch? They look you straight into your eyes and say, "The coffee around the corner is much better than yours."

"If you only stick to bagels and coffee you won't be here next year."

Is this honesty or rudeness? To this day I am still not sure about it. All I know their way of open communication takes a while to get used to. Of course, straight in your face is much better than behind your back. You know exactly what you are up against. Still, like I mentioned, it takes time to get used to.

During Queen's Day our coffee was praised. But we didn't see most of these guys again until the following year. The complaints I am talking about came from local drop-ins. Later on, I realized that these were the wrong kind of people to listen to. They never became part of our family. But hey, live and learn. At the early stages I didn't know better.

You can't please everybody was more than just a revelation, It was a lesson learned. How was it possible that I couldn't please all of Bussum? Strawberry Lounge was my creation, a personal extension of me. How could people not like me? Why didn't they like the product I offered or the atmosphere I was trying to create? It was beyond me. Quite frankly, I took it personally.

"If you don't like S.L. that means you don't like me," I thought. Does that make sense to you? Have you ever experienced something similar?

Thankfully, I grew a thick skin over time. How I wished to be personally detached from the business. Like a mother with her newborn, I didn't want to hear anything negative about my "baby". Like in a real pregnancy my project went through a gestation period and through painful labour pain before delivery. This project was based on love and devotion. Nobody had the right to say one bad word about it.

Whenever you take over an existing business and revamp it into something totally new, people will always leave their "pearls of wisdom". It takes time to weed out the old and attract the new crowd.

After we listened to these comments for a few days, our team came up with a referral strategy. Whenever somebody commented or requested something greasy, something more expensive or expansive, we referred them to the next snack bar or fancy bistro down the road. We didn't waste any time with anybody who didn't want to be here. With a friendly smile we offered them the chance to escape to what they really wanted. We made it easy for everybody to leave. Based on our conversations, the vibes we felt or comments we heard we either converted or referred. If I remember correctly, we referred a lot during the early days.

Our bagel only menu wasn't a success to begin with. What became a triumphant success was my policy to let everybody use our bathrooms free of charge. Can you believe Strawberry Lounge was the only shop in all of Bussum where you were allowed to pee regardless of being a guest or a passerby who was ready to burst? Something so simple and quite cheap (2 cents per flush) helped build our reputation and made us money, too. Most everybody stayed for a coffee or came back later.

Let me share with you one particular story:

A little boy came in and asked politely to let him use our restroom. "Of course, no problem, they are here to your left," he was told. He did his business, thanked me and left. A few minutes later his father came in and said, "Thank you for letting my son use your bathroom. I wanted to test you, if my son was allowed to use your washroom, I promised myself to come in and have coffee and cake with you." (This is Dutch directness.)

Regardless of all the comments and negative feedback received, I stuck to my guns. Strawberry Lounge became the first smoke-free hospitality venue in Bussum. The bagel, cake and coffee menu remained in place. My prices stayed at what I considered fair and didn't rise artificially just to fit into t'Gooi.

My crew had a kind word for everybody and we served coffee with gusto. We were truly building the business "one person at a time, one cup at a time."

From me to you:

Don't try to be for everyone, you will never be. Find the niche you want to cater to and don't worry about the rest. Do what you believe in, not what other people expect of you.

For some of our pickier visitors, we made the same coffee up to three times to top the competition and win them over. I had nothing to lose other than lots of milk, and a reputation to win. Our small crew took pride in getting it right for each individual. On one occasion I was so adamant, it took five attempts to get a personalized macchiato right. The whole ordeal left an impression and the lady in question became a regular and she still is.

By nature I am friendly, respectful and, hopefully, helpful. So were my two co-workers. To behave any other way at S.L. was out of the question.

Unfortunately, this wasn't the norm as Dominic and I experienced quite a few times as we toured the neighbourhood for some ideas. It is beyond me how members of the service industry could be cocky, arrogant, condescending or full of themselves.

I knew the whole idea of Strawberry Lounge was unique. We had it all, a fresh approach to cater towards children and their parents, our *uber*-friendly staff, the eclectic furniture mix, big pieces of cakes, customized coffee, free use of the WC and a fun, relaxed atmosphere. My sincere belief was Strawberry Lounge didn't have competition. Would I say something like that in front of our guests? Of course not. To me it was an open secret and I wanted everybody else to figure it out for themselves.

BUT, I DON'T KNOW ANYTHING ABOUT MARKETING. HOW CAN I REACH MY AUDIENCE?

Yes, this is a tough one. We all need to know how to reach our target audience. We need to connect with them, we want to offer them our products and keep them up to date.

For a hospitality business, the most logical solution is to put an ad into the paper, get a review and get a write up in the newspaper. We need our visitors to talk about us. They are the ones who spread the word for us.

Social media is another must in our fast and furious modern world.

I contacted our local paper to inform them about Strawberry Lounge. Sure enough they were interested about the new addition to Bussum. They sent a reporter only after I agreed to put four consecutive paid ads into their newspaper. So I did.

The reporter interviewed me and the article appeared in the paper. Did this do my business any good? Sure, people read about me. Did they walk in based on the story alone? No. Most of my visitors were referrals or accidental drop-ins. Would I recommend putting ads into the paper? Based on my experience, I must say "no". You see, shoppers don't necessarily walk into an empty bar just because they have seen your ad in the paper or read your story. However, they are more likely to walk into an empty bar after their friend or neighbour told them about this amazing bar, empty or not.

All our newcomers heard about S.L. from somebody else and wanted to check us out for themselves. We welcomed visitors from all around Holland to try our cheesecake. It was a big compliment and honour to hear that families travelled for an hour just to visit us. (Remember that Holland is a very small country, within one hour from Bussum you are at the border of Germany.) The money for the ads was wasted and another valuable lesson learned.

Here is a better idea of how to get a free story: Write a press release, starting with a fantastic headline. Invite the newspaper into your business and offer them freebies. Pitch your local radio station for your story.

Unfortunately, I never did what every great marketer recommends over and over again: Collect email addresses. I had a jar for business cards standing on the counter and most guests left their details but I never actively pursued this form of communication. We never had a Strawberry fan page. I never used Twitter. I don't like being bombarded with sales messages. In this sense, I am very far behind the expected norm.

Nobody ever "Liked" Strawberry Lounge on Facebook and honestly, I never really cared about it. I didn't have the time to sit on my computer. I had a business to run and a family to rear. If you wanted to get in touch with us you knew where to find us or you would call us.

So, how exactly did our guests find out about our special offers or events?

My wonderful, young strawberry staff did the tweeting and facebooking for me. The rest was all word of mouth.

I needed to reach the mothers and their children. How did that happen?

When you are a mother, you know lots of other mothers. That's just the way it is. We gravitate towards each other. We meet watching our children play sports; we meet picking up our loved ones from kindergarden or school. Oh yeah, we mothers know each other. Whenever we met, I mentioned Strawberry Lounge and invited the ladies along.

Fortunately, the mothers heard me calling and showed up. At the early stages a few curious moms visited us with their children. These moms needed to visit us only once and were seduced by easy-going manner and attitude. The ladies did what I secretly asked them to do – they spread the word. I have to hand it to us mothers. We are the perfect connectors. If we like something, we talk about it.

What is a lactating mother in most need of when she is out on the town? She needs a spot to breast feed her newborn. The Netherlands and Germany are very liberal in their breastfeeding policies. I didn't have a problem letting women feed their babies at the lounge and none of our other guests were bothered either. Lactating mothers found the "discreet, hidden behind a blanket-baby-sucking-version" of heaven. The word spread. Mothers brought their girlfriends, grandmas, acquaintances and eventually their boyfriends or husbands. We were on the right track to become a family affair.

After the summer months we already had a steady crowd of regulars. The connectors did a great job for my coffee shop.

From me to you:

If you offer something truly unique, people will do the work for you. They will use their social media skills to spread the good news for you. The advantage is, when it comes from somebody

else your own message is instantly much more credible. Anybody can blow his or her own horn. Let somebody else do it for you.

Find connectors to spread the word for you.

Here is an interesting fact I found out: Whenever I made a big deal about an upcoming event, I put up posters in the shop, in the bathrooms, I talked to our guests individually yet nobody showed up. Their excuse was, "We figured it would be too crowded and we wouldn't get a table anymore." Go figure this psychology out.

I CAN'T WORK ON SUNDAYS, IT'S OUR FAMILY DAY.

Sunday might be the day for rest and relaxation, to recharge your batteries and to enjoy time with family and friends. If you see Sunday as a potential moneymaking opportunity for your business, forget about treating it as holy.

After eight weeks of operation we realized Monday was the least profitable day of the whole week. Thankfully, my Canadian business mentors shared their secret for a profitable weekend: Their coffee bar was open on Sunday. Wow, that was a revelation.

In Bussum, nobody was open on the holiest day of the week. The grocery stores closed at 8 p.m. on Saturday and no businesses were open on Sunday. Only one bistro had its doors open on Sunday, and only during the summer months.

Dominic and I looked at Sunday from a business point of view. We could relate to families wanting to go out for a drink. With small children you want to stay close to home. Strawberry Lounge would be the perfect spot because it is only a short bike ride away from anywhere in Bussum. We decided to give it a shot.

As soon as Strawberry Lounge was open on Sundays we waved our own family day goodbye. Sunday became a moneymaking day for S.L. and a father's day for Dominic instead. Surprisingly enough, our boys were happy. They didn't have to go with their parents anymore doing stuff with them. Instead they could hang with their own friends.

Dominic read or did upkeep on our house. As soon as this routine was established everybody was happy and Sunday life became very relaxed indeed. Mondays were now free to do the banking, shopping for home and S.L. and our boys could eat lunch at home with their mom.

It took less time than expected to make Sunday one of our most popular days of the week.

The decision to be open on Sunday made a huge impact on our family life. I sacrificed our family time in order for other families to have somewhere to spend their family time together. It was difficult to get the staff committed to work on a regular basis on Sundays. They all wanted to be with their friends and doing whatever fun things young women like doing. Therefore, it was my turn to do the shifts most Sundays.

WHAT IS HAPPENING?

Something strange happened, quite unexpectedly, when we expanded our circle of parents with children to teenagers.

When or how exactly it happened, I am still unclear about. All of a sudden high school teenagers discovered us. It must have been three months into operation when one of the mothers brought her teenage daughter. One sip of our caramel flavoured coffee shake and a bite of the irresistible cheesecake was all it took to get her hooked.

Teenagers and mothers are the two most powerful groups of connectors for which marketers can wish. Teenagers spread the news as fast as they can talk. When the first teenaged girls arrived, I thought it was a fluke but the girls kept coming. To this day the young ladies still invade Strawberry Lounge by the masses. Without further ado, my little coffee business extended its target group to "sweet sixteeners". Don't ask me how or why but Strawberry Lounge hit the nail straight on the head.

The one group who stayed away from us was adolescent boys (Until recently Dutch law allowed teenagers from the age of sixteen to drink beer). In their eyes we were not cool enough. The young men would rather hang out at the local pub with other like-minded souls than drink coffee and shakes with the girls and family folks. Can you blame them?

I DON'T HAVE A USP (UNIQUE SELLING POINT)

Of course you have. Sometimes it is your friendly personality, your excellent service or your amazing product. And sometimes it is even more. Don't worry; you may find your USP quite by chance.

After five months in business Marcello quit, to be replaced by Anne. In Anne, I found a gem every business owner dreams about. She was loyal, hard working, honest, had a wonderful personality, and was a quick learner. As if that wasn't enough, she combined all these attributes with perfect teeth and attractive looks. Anne happened to "hang" after school with her friends at S.L. Eventually, she asked me for a job – which I gladly gave to her. Anne stayed with me right to the end, until Strawberry Lounge was sold. We celebrated our first party together; we celebrated my farewell party together.

She became my official graphic designer. Her curvy handwriting was perfect for writing the display chalkboard. In the years to come we made a perfect team to organize and decorate the Strawberry for our special events. Not only her handwriting and work ethics made Anne attractive. Most of all, Anne was the perfect connector. She found ways to deliver and spread the news via her vast social networks. (It doesn't take much to impress me.) She was a gem. Thanks to her, I could also recruit a few of her friends to work at the lounge.

Within five months of operation, Anne helped to plan our first ever, themed Saturday for the lounge. It was October, a perfect excuse to celebrate Halloween. The Dutch know what Halloween is but nobody really cares or takes advantage of it. When we started to decorate, I discovered another one of Anne's talents. She was very creative. With a few slingers, balloons, aluminum foil and a spray can for the windows we transformed Strawberry Lounge into a highly competitive and utterly attractive Halloween location.

Not merely satisfied with the transformation of our location, we decided to go with the theme and roamed through fancy dress shops. But instead of spending money on a costume we plundered our own wardrobes and discovered a little fantasy can go a long way.

Our guests were greeted and served by "Captain Jack Sparrow" and "Cruella Deville". We served eyeball cookies (made by Anne), witches lemonade, and blue lattes. Our latte lovers were shockingly surprised when their tongues turned and stayed blue. Oops, we added too much food colouring.

By the end of the day we had a success on our hands. Our theme was well received, our efforts were appreciated and most of all we made everybody laugh. I was the owner so I sold the whole idea of Halloween with gusto, enthusiasm, pirate boots and knife-through-my-skull headpiece. Halloween stayed a fixed item on the annual events calendar for years to come.

After Halloween, the party bug infected us. We loved our set-up and costumes so much that we couldn't wait for the next big date to come along. If we wanted to sparkle, we had one last chance that year. Christmas time was our big opportunity to bring magic into the lives of our newfound friends.

Yet again, we busied ourselves to transform the lounge. This time around it resembled the grotto of Santa Claus. We cut glitzy stars, bought cotton balls to simulate snowflakes and stuck them to the windows. We replaced the big pictures on the wall with massive, long garlands and decorated them with tasteful Christmas ornaments. We put up a Christmas tree. And last but not least, we hung mistletoe from the ceiling. Our first Christmas period was a controlled orgy of random kisses under the mistletoe. Once again, we heard cheers, laughter and received lots of kisses.

Here is an idea for you: Imagine what will happen if you hang some mistletoe directly above your cash register … just saying.

As a special treat to my ever-growing visitor base, I organized a Christmas-spectacle, including carol singers, a fire on the terrace for marshmallow roasting, free mulled wine and Christmas cake.

To add more authenticity to the theme we dressed as angels in white outfits or evening dresses. We even strapped on angel wings. Working with wings in the small kitchen was a difficult and challenging undertaking, however, they were great for catching attention and charming comments. How many times have you been served by an angel in a coffee shop? I bet not very often. Our guests were in awe. The idea was so simple, so inexpensive and oh, so effective. It was another round of cheers and laughter when the angels flew from table to table to deliver their goodies.

The Strawberry was overcrowded during our first-ever Christmas celebration. Guests and accidental passersby gathered outside to listen to the carol singers. They followed the singers inside to listen to another burst of a Capella and funky versions of much-loved classics. Once again, we were congratulated on our efforts and complimented on our looks.

How much did all this cost? In the case of the Christmas celebration, it was as much as ten bags of marshmallows, one sack of kindling, one sack of firewood and free flowing mulled wine and cakes for the singers. Our carol singers were recruited from our own school band.

The old saying, "Ask and you shall receive," still holds truth. Sometimes you just need to get over yourself, take a deep breath and ask for what you want. I offered free food and drinks in return for the talents of our singers.

Try it. Ask for a favour and be sure to offer something in return. You will be pleasantly surprised to find out how many organizations, groups or individuals are genuinely willing to help out a start-up business. Once again, please make sure you offer a small token of gratitude.

The Christmas celebration became another fixed feature in our events calendar. After seven months in business I found my Unique Selling Point (USP) for Strawberry Lounge. It was themed parties on a Saturday, presented hand-in-hand with the appropriate costumes and food items.

This whole development was neither planned nor was it calculated. Believe me, the business plan didn't even mention the word party. It just happened.

Because our parties weren't planned years in advance it all felt quite natural to our guests and to us. It was an extension of the core business. Our visitors were surprised over and over again but didn't get the feeling they were part of a hard-core promotional machine.

To make a good thing even better, I came full circle with my childhood memories. My birthday is in February, a time of year too cold to host a birthday party outside. February is also carnival season in Germany. That made it a perfect excuse to host a fancy dress party for my birthday year after year. As CEO (Chief Events Organizer) for the Strawberry business I could relive these wonderful childhood years over and over again.

The whole process of planning and organizing a themed day is something I love doing. It wasn't a problem or an embarrassment to choose a ridiculous or funny outfit, as long as it was appropriate to the theme and to our guests. As the owner, I set the example and expected the same from my strawberries. And let me tell you this, the girls always delivered. Most times their costumes and make-up were ten times better and more creative than mine.

During the next year we found another event suitable to celebrate and dress up for. We chose International Woman's Day to honour women the world over. In order to represent all different types of our wonderful species we dressed up as housewives, businesswomen, students or mothers. This event also offered a perfect excuse to serve coffee in one of my favourite outfits.

I took the liberty to represent a stay at home, "it's my lazy day off" kind of woman and represented her – in my pyjamas. From the laughs I received I can tell you, it was another success. From the comfort level of wearing pyjamas, it was an even bigger success. What can I say? Nothing is too tight and nothing pinches. You don't need to worry about bra lines or underwear show. If you add a comfy pair of bath slippers, the near-heaven experience is guaranteed. If I had my say, I would introduce an "International Pyjama Day." Try it one day.

While I am on the pyjama topic I have to share another costume idea with you. This one is another head turner. Let me call it the "Cleaning Goddess". Squeeze into your skimpy black dress and black pantyhose. Wrap a wonderful long, fake pearl necklace around your neck and for goodness sake; remember to wear long rubber gloves. As footwear I recommend the tried and tested bath slippers again. As I said earlier, they offer comfort and freedom. But here comes the cherry on top of the cake. If the length of your hair permits put curlers in, leave them in and wear them with pride.

The best comment I received wearing this outfit came from a lady called Anne-Meike. She arrived thirty minutes before closing time, looked me up and down, didn't flinch and looked me straight in the eyes. In a matter-of-fact speaking voice she said, "Gee Christina has nobody told you yet? You forgot to take your curlers out this morning." We both exploded in laughter.

This costume idea is most suitable for the female reader. However, I am pretty convinced any motivated man will come up with a comparable equivalent.

TIME TO PARTY

Music is a fantastic medium to conquer the hearts of your guests, young or old alike. Here are a few ideas of how we used music to boogie our way from the espresso machine to the tables:

Return of the 80s

This is a fantastic theme to let your creativity come out fully. Don't we all have a little bit of Madonna, Cindy Lauper, Boy George or David Bowie inside us? This is your perfect opportunity to shine and sparkle in your best ever costume. Duran Duran, Heaven 17, here we come.

Revisit the 70s

This day is fantastic for the outfits alone. The music is memorable and popular. My personal tip is to stick to the original versions. They are much better than all the remixes around. With slight embarrassment I must admit I love the band ABBA still to this day. Our 70s day gave me a legitimate excuse to blast their music out all day long. (Check out our photos on www.themotherpreneur.com. What do you think of my white boots?)

Step into Grease Lightning Mode, The 50s

Check out flea markets or thrift stores for a petticoat and a black leather jacket, slap some grease into your hair and off you go. We served hot dogs and ice cream sodas for this particular fun event.

How about an Elvis Presley day, or a Rock'a Billy day? I know you are creative.

Create a Cocktail Party

One year I hired live musicians. We had a saxophone and big contra bass player who seduced us with their sexy tunes for a perfectly, lazy summer afternoon. If you don't want to spend the money, use your boom box instead.

We decided to offer four easy to mix cocktails (e.g. Mojito, Tequila Sunrise, Bacardi Cola, and Salty Dog). To make the atmosphere as authentic as possible we borrowed cocktail shakers, put on swanky, knee length cocktail dresses, added a bow tie and slipped into knee high boots. If you don't have an alcohol license, don't despair. Serving non-alcoholic mixed drinks will do the trick, too. It is more about the idea of creating an atmosphere and setting the stage for something different.

Karaoke

This is another, unexpected, gimmick for a coffee shop. Karaoke is mainly offered by pubs and bars, not by a coffee shop. Here is one word of caution for the set-up: Keep the volume at minimal and medium. If it's too loud some people will stay away, and some will never leave the stage. One year I hired a fully professional sound system including the screen, Top-40 CD collections and two microphones. It wasn't cheap but we had it from Friday till Monday and got full use out of it.

Country and Western

Jonny Cash, Dolly Parton, Garth Brooks plus friends were entertaining us from early morning until late in the afternoon. We created our own cowboy outfits without having to buy anything new. For this day I even made "my girls" study a line dance routine. Did we do line dancing in the shop? You bet we did.

To the embarrassment of our guests we invited them to join the line. As so often in life, we only needed to persuade the first person to join us before the rest tagged along.

Apart from the music theme we surprised our guests with a theme based around a country. The most obvious choice was:

German Day

German Evergreens were blasting from the boom box, our dresses were prepped with push up bras (think Oktoberfest in Bavaria). By command of their CEO (me) the strawberry girls had to tie their long hair into braids. It was as authentic as we could make it. Surely, you couldn't find it better anywhere in Germany. The day before I cooked, peeled and created bowls full of real potato salad. I found German sausages at the wholesaler, baked trays of plum cake and served it with freshly whipped cream. The whole meal could be washed down with Becks Bier or Melitta kaffee (two German brands).

Spain

For the Spanish Day, we decorated the lounge with yellow and red crepe paper. We baked tortillas the night before and served them either hot or cold. Our outfits resembled flamenco dresses, borrowed from willing friends. When Julio and Enrique Iglesias started singing (sadly on CDs only) our lady visitors melted, happily munching on their tuna tortilla. I don't know what the men thought about it but as supportive boyfriends or husbands they put on brave faces, making the most of their situation.

A Disney Day

There is Disneyland in California and Disney World in Florida - therefore I put Disney into the category of countries.

Stick to the cute Disney characters and you have a success at hand. The children, in particular, will love you. And if you impress the children, their parents will love you even more.

How about a Japanese Sushi theme or a Chinese Noodle day? There are so many countries that all we need to do is pick and choose. Think about France (cheese, baguettes), Sweden (fish), Belgium (chocolates to eat and to drink), England (tea, greasy fish and chips), Turkey (pitas, kebabs) etc.

For my own inconvenience, I persuaded myself to offer a theme at least once a month. Much can be said about being consistent and staying sharp in business. I put myself under constant pressure to come up with something new, different and exciting. The phrase, "it's the time of the month again" took on a different meaning for me.

All the added baking, cooking and decorating took longer than it should have. And yes, on occasion I wished we hadn't done it. Nevertheless, at the end of each day it was always worth the sweat. Big smiles and laughter can make up for a lot of inconvenience.

Another event I liked to organize was Sunday Brunch.

We set up a long table along one of our walls, filled it with sandwiches, soups, cakes and salads and offered is as a self-serve buffet.

It all came together. These years of operation were like a journey into self-discovery. I figured out what I love more than making coffee and spoiling our guests: It was party planning driven by my quirky desire to surprise our unwitting guests. At times it was so much fun that I even daydreamed about another career. I saw myself as a wedding planner. That would give me lots of organizing and planning to do. Right here is a good time to remind you of the old saying, "Be careful what you wish for, it might actually come true..."

It is all about having fun. Running your own business can and should be more than escaping survival mode day in and day out. The bottom line is, the more fun you have, the more fun your guests have. The more fun they have the longer they will stay with you, spend money and will spread the word. You set the example, you set the mood, and you create an atmosphere.

Don't worry if it has never been done before and don't worry about what people might say about you. Do you know when your business is dead? When nobody talks about you anymore. Let people talk and give them something to talk about. It doesn't matter if it's positive or negative; people need to talk about you. Why do you think Justin Bieber is doing so well? Or Rihanna, for that matter? They give their fans and the press something to talk about. They are constantly in the news, regardless of the topic.

ONCE YOU START THERE IS NO STOPPING

In October 2006, our USP was born. This in itself was a fantastic discovery. To make a good thing even better, we also had our first request to host a private party. The request came from one of our regular guests who wanted to celebrate the baptism of her daughter with us.

Of course, I said yes. I had no idea what was on her mind but how hard could it be to organize a lunch for twelve? For our first formal reservation we created an extended menu. We catered towards the wishes of the hostess and added soups, salads and vegetarian choices. One side of Strawberry Lounge was set aside with a beautifully set table. This happy family get-together was our "live advertisement" for the day. And boy, did this do the trick. From that day onwards the reservations started to come in.

We catered for girls-get-togethers, birthday parties, anniversaries, family reunions and Sweet 16 parties. Instead of a "hen night" we had a "hen afternoon". The bride-to-be loved Bailey's (sinfully good Irish liqueur) so we surprised her with a whole new menu, specially designed for her party. All dishes included a shot of Bailey's in one form or another.

We took advantage of Valentine's Day, Mother's Day and Father's Day. We offered something fun and different for each celebration. It was always the small stuff that made these days extraordinary. For example, we gave away roses to each mother on Mother's Day, and we set our tables in pink for Valentine's Day. We also used the ceiling to create a nice backdrop for an event. Depending on the season and event we had butterflies, flowers, bees, spiders, stars or hearts dangling from the ceiling.

Nothing is more inviting than a beautifully set table, fresh flowers and your "Sunday-best" tea or coffee set. This special tea set was stored at home, safely hidden in the furthest corner of our kitchen cupboard. My lovely expensive English tea set saw the light of day only on special occasions. In other words, never. I finally convinced myself of the fact that beautiful "English Rose" had better use at Strawberry Lounge than at home. With a heavy heart, I finally decided to transport it across the streets to make it part of our special occasion events. Our female guests in particularly appreciated this gesture. Oh, what joy a tea set can bring. With so much appreciation it was hard to worry too long about my own emotional attachment to the cups and saucers.

Needless to say my beloved tea set immigrated with us to Canada. Here in Vancouver it is safely tucked away in the furthest corner of our kitchen cupboard, waiting for the special occasion.

I KNOW NOTHING ABOUT HOSTING PARTIES

As a general rule I said yes to every proposal I received, regardless of whether I had done it before or not. I always figured, "Why not? This is a great opportunity to learn something new."

Isn't it an honour to be asked to be part of someone's special something? To me, it is. I felt so humbled and excited to be trusted to create something magical at Strawberry Lounge. To me it is a privilege to be chosen from all the other locations on offer. I never had a standard price or standard features for an event. Every party, every get-together was individually designed and priced.

How can you make a special occasion even more special?

I always asked my guest to describe their perfect party to me. I wanted to know exactly what they had in mind, how many guests they expected, what they wanted to eat, how long they wanted to stay, what lay-out they preferred (buffet style or individual servings). Did they bring their own baby-sitters (if applicable), would they bring their own music, and if not, what kind of music do they like? What are their favourite colours and flowers?

These last few items might be meaningless, however, they can make all the difference in the world to your guests. It showed them you listened and you cared.

We greeted our guests with a handshake, a hug or a kiss. We tried to remember as many names as possible from their friends. These are a few of the "small stuff" things we did to make Strawberry Lounge extraordinary.

Later on, one of our guests asked if we could make High Tea for her party. Okay, how difficult could it be to whip up a few cucumber sandwiches? I said yes and once again, we had another prominent item on our menu.

One mother asked if she could celebrate her daughter's birthday with us. Guess what my answer was? We ended up making handcrafts with the girls and decorated cup cakes. Do you remember when I told you we mothers are great connectors?

After our first successful inauguration of a children's party this particular mother did her best to talk about our new service. The word spread faster than one could imagine and voila, from that day onwards I found myself in the lucrative market of hosting children parties. Hosting a party with us was a guaranteed ticket back into their own tidy house.

Our repertoire included T-shirt painting, playing old-fashioned games outside and inside, decorating cup cakes, cooking, painting flowerpots or doing any other sort of handy craft. An absolute hit became our "Disco-Pizza-Cake-party".

Earlier in the book I mentioned my previous life as fitness instructor. Being an aerobics instructor teaches you, among other things, to move and speak freely in front of an audience. I must admit I still get stage fright and the only ingredient to cure it is music. My brain is hardwired to perform well with music.

Thirteen years is a long time to build a repertoire of moves for young and not so young. These moves are still stored in my brain. Push 'start' on any device and they came back to life.

Now picture the following: Fifteen young girls (and the odd boy at times) started their birthday bash with a sing-along, dancing, wiggling, stomping dance routine. The birthday girl normally brought her own music. I made up a routine on the spot and the whole party followed, including parents.

Totally hyped, our young chefs had to cut their own toppings (mozzarella cheese, vegetables, and meats) and had to cut lots more veggies for a big bowl of salad. I always bought the pizza bases. While the pizza was baking the table needed to be cleared, cleaned and set for dinner.

That was done quickly and we ended up playing games. If we stayed inside we played musical chairs, balloon dancing or musical statues. If we went outside we played running games mostly. It was the perfect way to run off steam and to work up an appetite.

Do you want to know what the parents did? Depending on the age of their child they stayed with me and lent a helping hand. Or they left the whole party in my own capable hands and picked up the birthday group later. Sometimes we even had an after-party with all the grown-ups, drinking to the well being of the birthday girl.

We didn't just entertain kiddies on their birthday. Here are a few other examples of how our not so young guests wanted to spend their birthday at Strawberry Lounge:

One huge Italian fan wanted an Italian-style brunch. After roaming through Mediterranean cookbooks we designed a lunch serving pizza, bruschetta, mozzarella-tomato-basilica sticks and figs wrapped in Parma ham. It became as Italian as we could imagine, considering it was created and served by the German-Dutch crew. As an extra surprise to her we made sure all the drinks served were in the colours of the Italian flag: red wine, white wine and cold green spinach soup.

We had a 40s birthday party where twenty-five ladies cooked a fabulous, three-course menu from scratch. We had champagne, wine and beer flowing until deep into the night. It was spectacular to experience what a bunch of friends can cook up with basic ingredients. The music was blasting, they were dancing in between whipping up a perfect Tiramisu, singing along to Top 40 Hits and happily chatting the night away.

Another lady wanted to host a dance party to celebrate her 40th birthday with us. For this occasion we transformed our daytime operation into a nightclub. Her sixty friends let their hair down and boogied the night away until three o'clock in the morning. This was the only night party I ever hosted. I did it for the experience only. I prefer to sleep at night and operate during daylight hours only.

The really big money-spinners were privately hosted anniversaries, baby showers or birthday parties for up to fifty guests. For these occasions the host rented Strawberry Lounge for a fraction of the day. Anne and I loved these get-togethers because it gave us the perfect stage on which to shine as a fantastic team. We did it all: the transformation from lounge to party head quarters; everything from the personal greetings at the door to taking coats and orders. We were so crowded that simple tasks like restocking the buffet, clearing dishes and grabbing drinks forced us to hold in our tummies, throw up our arms and slide through the cracks in the masses.

We had fifty square meters packed with enthusiastic, chatty visitors, all indulging in our cake buffet, drinking coffee or tea by the litres (or whatever their host ordered). One word can't describe these wonderful events, but three can: Fun, mad, rewarding.

For peace of mind, I made sure all preparations were done at least fifteen minutes before arrival time of the honoured guests. That still gave us enough time to make last minute adjustments or changes.

Which one of all the parties hosted was my absolute highlight in five and a half years in business? Without hesitation I can say it was the wedding reception for Nanda and Kees plus their 100 guests. I got a glimpse of what it would take to become a wedding planner. Being trusted with this honour, we pulled everything imaginable out of the closet. The whole preparation was a combined effort of the in-laws and the Strawberry crew. During our pre-wedding talks, I found out everything I needed to know in regards to set-up, arrival time, special wishes, and favourite colour of the bride and favourite flowers of the groom.

Within a day we transformed our cheerful coffee lounge into a white-pink palace fit for a queen and king. Big hearts made of builders foam replaced our big pictures. We covered our green Christmas garland with pink and white crepe paper and placed it as a portal in front of our door. As a surprise present from us to the happy couple we organized a singer/guitar duo to perform love songs for the lovebirds.

What made this event so special? It wasn't just the occasion or the amount of guests we had to cater for. The true reason why this reception remains an unforgettable event was the fact that bride and groom plus their 100 guests showed up forty minutes earlier than our agreed arrival time. (I can forgive them for overestimating their allotted "I do" time. For both of them it is their first marriage.)

Within three years of business we built a reputation as a cozy, family friendly coffee bar with kick-ass service and a good price-quality structure. We built a loyal circle of followers, which expanded by the day.

It goes without saying it wouldn't be possible without my wonderful staff, the Strawberry girls. Here is another confession for you: Marcello was the one and only man who had the privilege of working as a

"Strawberry". Later on it came down to lack of applicants and even later, lack of job openings.

I HAVE NO CLUE HOW TO FIND GOOD STAFF

By now you know starting your own business is a challenging undertaking. On top of your daily uncertainties of "how many people will I have today and how much money will I make," you need to stay tuned to the wishes and demands of your own family.

I knew Ulrica and Marcello as friends before we started working together. They were both gracious with their time. They shared their fantastic energy and enthusiasm with me to help me endure the start-up pain. I trusted them both completely and we worked very well together as a team.

The problems started when we got busier. After I figured out the basics of running the lounge, the next challenge was to figure out the employment strategy. Early on I knew I couldn't afford a manager and later on I didn't want one. Right from the start something unforeseen happened: I fell in love with Strawberry Lounge. This love transformed me into a control freak.

Dear friend, please be aware of this treacherous, all encompassing, soul-eating phenomena. Do you know what I am talking about? I was so adamant about figuring everything out by myself. I wanted and needed to learn everything. I had to have my fingers involved in every aspect of the coffee bar. Strawberry Lounge became, not only my fourth baby, it became my alter ego.

Ulrica wanted to get back to her old teaching job. Marcello got itchy feet after the first hurdles were successfully mastered. Both of them did their deeds, now their time was up. It was up to me to find their replacements. Right when Marcello was ready to leave Anne walked into my life. Thanks to Anne I was able to recruit some of her girlfriends who stayed loyal to S.L. for years to come. As a result, the turnover in staff was minimal.

Once I tried to recruit via an ad in the paper. Only one girl, aged sixteen, applied. I had more luck putting a note on the front door or recruiting my guests. I did it twice and it worked out very well. We had a constant stream of young girls asking for a part-time job during the summer holiday or the weekends. Therefore, I had a few girls on the stand-by list in case of a real staff shortage.

HOW THE HECK DO I DO INTERVIEWS?

During the interview process I always relied on my gut feeling and first impressions. Let me warn you, first impressions are deceiving. More important than looks are the vibes you receive from that person. Talk is cheap; it always is. Most applicants will make themselves sound better than they actually are.

If I liked the girl, I needed to see her in action. The best resume doesn't mean anything if you can't perform under pressure or if you are not a people person. Anybody with logical understanding can be taught how to make coffee, how to operate a cash register, how to cut cakes, or how to prepare bagels.

What nobody can teach is passion, compassion or to have a personality. These are traits that come from within. When it comes to working in the hospitality industry you either have what it takes to be a success or you don't. The person in service with the brightest personality gets most of the tips. It is that simple.

Whenever one of the girls agreed for a try-out, I always paid them. If we both liked the experience we signed a payroll contract, otherwise, it was *hasta la vista*. I set two training days aside to show and explain the working procedures involved. We had special sessions in the evening where we mixed our coffees and practiced making froth.

Before a big event we all came together for a formal meeting. Otherwise, it was ad-hoc (on the spot) management style for me. Thankfully, I never had a trust issue with any of my staff. I never ever considered they would steal from me, so they never did. I knew they would give a muffin or cookie to one of their friends during my absence. However, that comes with the territory of working in a coffee shop. During their shifts the girls were allowed to eat what they wanted during appropriate quiet times. Stealing from me was never one of my concerns. I had a very different concern: How well did the girls behave when I wasn't around? Did they deliver the same quality service I do? Did they turn the lights off in the cellar? Did they close the freezer doors? Did they check the washrooms? Did they go out of their way to make our guests comfortable?

At the very beginning I was convinced only a mother could be a rightful representation of Strawberry Lounge. Not true. From my own experience I can testify that it doesn't matter if you are 18 or 38 when it comes to working in the service industry. Remember, you either have this special "something" or you don't. After years of working with the young and the not so young ladies I came to the following conclusion: With the odd exception and with all due respect, I prefer working with the young ones. Enthusiasm, big hearts and loads of energy easily replaced their lack of motherly experience.

During operation time I had six girls on my payroll. All of them were paid more than what the law required. Does money buy loyalty? Of course to a certain extent, it does. Money is a good motivator. However, respect and fair treatment weigh equally high when it comes down to keeping your employees happy.

One of the advantages of being your own boss is choosing your own people; you are able to choose individuals you like to work with.

Years back, I often felt like one big softy because so many times I felt I was too nice to my staff. Whenever something bothered me, I had a hard time delivering my speech as their employer. Today I learned my lessons and approach any kind of conflict without hesitation and with full gusto. I learned that if something bothers me I need to get it off my chest, straight away.

In business, we women need to behave like men: Bring it out in the open, fight and get it over with. Arguments should be about business and not on personal issues. Sadly, I have to admit I wasn't the most skilled negotiator or diplomatic manager back then.

After I learned to be more precise, direct and honest (the Dutch way), I learned so many facts about managing people. For example, if personalities clash I wouldn't let these opposites work together anymore. I asked myself these two questions: Which person harms my business? Who adds to the business? On that simple basis I let someone go or stay.

I was worried about being too nice but the girls always stayed longer, came earlier, always did more than what I asked for; they went out of their way to help out. In a way, being a softie worked out just fine.

My Strawberry team was a fun mix of young students and not so young mothers. The girls very lovely, they were a bunch of well brought up, well-behaved Bussum girls. On an annual basis we opened our house for a summer party, a Christmas dinner and a silly games night in.

From me to you:

If you are in the fortunate position to employ people, please remember: Being older doesn't mean being better. In our industry it is all about having a likeable personality and an ability to learn and to relate to our guests.

Without our staff we couldn't run our business. We should all treat and pay them well.

HOW CAN I ASK FOR WHAT I WANT? ISN'T IT RUDE TO ASK?

The new, modern, online business entrepreneur gives free contents away. The online marketer solves a few problems first then asks for a sale. In the conventional business world we should build a relationship first then ask for what we want. This is all good and nice to know, today.

I didn't know about these codes of conducts a few years back. Mind you, I always tell our sons to ask for what they want. How else would they get what they want or need? Our children at a young age can get away with murder when it comes to plainly speaking and asking for what they want. And so can we. All we need to do is muster the courage to ask the right people in the right position.

The summer of 2006 was a hot one. I remember my frustration when I saw all the children with their parents going to the ice cream store around the corner instead of having a fruit shake at Strawberry Lounge. We lost out on so much potential business that it made me want to cry. I didn't cry but I became rather frustrated, to say the least. The most logical solution was to sell ice cream as well.

As logical and straight forward the idea might seem, it was easier said than done. First, I never planned on selling ice cream. Strawberry Lounge didn't have an ice cream freezer, and second, we had no ice cream to sell. I had this weird pride in my head not to sell any pre-packed ice creams. If I was to do it, I wanted to become a serious competition to the proper ice cream store.

One morning Dominic had heard enough of my complaining. "Stop speculating. Why don't you call "De Hoop" and ask if you could sell their ice cream?" Did I just hear this right? Was he joking or serious?

"De Hoop" is the most famous, best ice cream maker in the whole of t'Gooi. Thousands of ice cream lovers plus numerous awards for best-tasting ice cream over the years can testify to this statement. De Hoop is an established family business for over 72 years. It is *the* Mecca in ice cream production and consumption. Their customers are willing to stand in line for an hour to purchase three scoops of creamy delight.

Hmmm, let me check the statistics for you. Strawberry Lounge opened its doors two months ago. The Lounge didn't have a name, a reputation or a customer base yet.

De Hoop, on the other hand was a well-established, successful family owned business with over seventy years of experience. Their experience and reputation are unlike any others. They have a customer base most of us are dreaming about.

Do you see why I was so hesitant? This was a venture against all odds. Did I take the plunge? Yes, I made the call, once again with sweaty palms. I called the owner herself to find out if she would sell me her goods. My heart was racing when I rang the number. Caroline Kooij, ice cream-maker par excellence and owner listened to my introduction, the rehearsed pitch, and thought for a while. While she was thinking we had a nice chit-chat about my business. At the end of the conversation, Caroline agreed to sell me her ice cream.

To this day I still wonder why she said yes to my proposal. One thing I will bet on, she didn't do it for the money. Eventually, I stopped wondering or analyzing. Instead, I enjoyed the wonderful feeling of accomplishment. Fortunately, the price per litre ice cream was very reasonable. Unfortunately, the ice-salon didn't have a delivery system in place. Not a big deal, we (Dominic and I) agreed to pick it up ourselves. Driving back and forth was a small price to pay to have the opportunity to sell their fabulous, famous product.

With the ice cream deal under my belt there was one more item to organize: The ice cream display fridge. Google was the magic word for anything I needed. The universe struck again. For a very good price I could purchase a second hand one from a neighbouring city. And this is how the Strawberry story continued. Within a week we were in the ice cream business to profit from the hot summer days.

From me to you:

Ask for what you want. The answer can only be Yes or No. Don't be afraid to ask for the best.

Another example of bowing to demand was to serve toasties (melted cheese). Toasties are the staple food of the Dutch kitchen and everyone loves them – and I mean, everyone.

For the longest time I refused to put them on our menu because they are too common. Every hospitality location in Bussum offered toasties. That was reason enough for me not to offer them. I wanted to stick to my bagel menu. Big mistake.

As soon as we became known for our child friendliness the requests for toasties increased. Everyday new requests came in. It seemed like everybody wanted to eat toasties at Strawberry Lounge. How much longer could I say no to this demand? Once we decided to put them on our menu they became our biggest seller in a very short period of time. Quite often we even ran out of bread due to the unprecedented demand.

SUCCESSFUL, HAPPY AND MAKING MONEY, WHAT'S NEXT?

My original idea was to set up Strawberry Lounge, train a bunch of workers, work for two days a week on the floor (to keep in touch with what is going on) and then work exclusively behind the scenes. This is called working "on" the business instead of "in" the business.

The short-term goal was to establish S.L. as a successful, profitable business in Bussum and surrounding area. The long-term goal was to establish a S.L. in ten medium-size cities. Unfortunately, the one variable I didn't account for was love. I told you earlier, I fell in love with my enterprise.

Strawberry Lounge became Christina.

Christina became Strawberry Lounge.

Freedom and independence are two small words with big meanings. They are aphrodisiacs for the soul. Making money is an addiction, even if I didn't make much at the beginning. A long time ago I was hooked on physical exercise, now I was hooked on creating a "dream come true".

Since opening month, Strawberry Lounge experienced a curve in income. Every week got better; every month got better. I don't quite remember when the business broke even but it was after only a few months. As I wrote earlier, the status quo doesn't exist. A business can only go up or down. If you want your business to expand there are two ways of doing so.

The business can expand horizontally or diagonal. Horizontal diversification means it will expand to different locations. Diagonal diversification refers to staying where you are but adding to the existing business model. Examples are to offer longer opening hours, to add an extra day open or to offer special lunches or dinners – in short, to open up your business to new opportunities. In my case, it would be to open Mondays or to extend the evening hours and include a dinner menu.

There is nothing wrong with being and remaining small. Just go with the flow and avoid stagnation. At one point I offered free WIFI to make S.L. even more attractive to the teenagers doing homework or other guests wanting to check online activities. Having the extra service added to my monthly expenses but its attraction was immense.

One of our regular ladies suggested that we should offer a free book exchange. From an expense point of view it was a brilliant idea – it cost nothing. Strawberry Lounge had enough space available to add a small (second-hand) bookshelf where everybody could drop off used books. Depending on the books available we had a flourishing exchange going. Once an author approached me to host a book presentation and I gladly offered him Strawberry Lounge for the evening.

Jill, an American lady, was looking for a spot to teach Dutch children the basics of English. She figured S.L. would be the perfect location for a lesson once a week. Together we agreed to offer the class every Saturday morning before official opening time (9 a.m.). Our door was open and quite often we had other early birds in need of a caffeine fix. They marched right in and I served them all. These unaware drop-ins found themselves surrounded by singing, clapping, stomping or dancing toddlers. At these times we were often mistaken for a day care centre.

After three years in business I found myself at a crossroads. Should I expand, sell, or work to make S.L. the most popular coffee lounge in the area? Being the control freak I had become, I saw the goal of ten Strawberry Lounges slipping. How on earth could I control each and every one of them? This character flaw stopped me from expansion.

Another reason not to go "global" was our personal circumstance. Dominic and I both have "itchy feet". We both are always on the lookout for something new to explore, to learn and to move to.

Here in Bussum we lived in a town and a country where we knew we didn't belong. None of us had any family roots or obligations here (other than by choice). Our minds and feet became more restless by the day. Over and over we discussed our situation and asked ourselves, "Why do we live in one of the most crowded countries in the world where none of us actually speaks and understands the language? What are we here for? And more importantly, why are we still here?"

We both ran successful businesses but at the bottom of our hearts we knew one thing: To reach our maximal potential we had to live and work in an English-speaking country. We had to get out of there – soon. Otherwise, our children would be too old to make the move. If we left we had an awesome chance to settle down somewhere new without doing too much damage control.

We decided to take action and move on. After weighing the pros and cons of various countries we decided to apply for our immigration to Canada. We were ready to move from one of the smallest countries in the world to the second biggest one. With our application on the way an expansion of Strawberry Lounge was out of the question. We didn't know how long the immigration process would take and once approved, how much time we had to pack our belongings.

For the unforeseeable future we were left in limbo. The only options left were selling S.L. or staying put to make it the hippest, most popular spot in the area. I decided on option two. From that point onwards it was party, party, party. With the basic lounge business well established I could concentrate on hosting more events. Metaphorically speaking, the coffee lounge business was the daily bread and butter on the table, hosting parties was the dessert.

TIME TO SELL

The clock was ticking and it was time to put S.L. up for sale. We wanted to make another major move. I had two options to sell "my baby". Option One was to sell The Strawberry Corporation by myself and Option Two was to engage an agent on my behalf. To get the ball rolling I decided on the first choice.

When the news of the sale became public I was bombarded with well-meaning business advice. As always, everybody voiced his or her strongest personal opinion and feelings about my decision. The one thing everybody agreed on was the fact that "Strawberry Lounge is unsellable." The other encouraging statements were "Strawberry Lounge needs Christina to stay a success", and "The Strawberry Lounge without Christina will lose its attraction and popularity".

Fortunately, by this time I was used to the "Dutch freedom of speech". On closer inspection I noticed one characteristic among all these "know-it-alls". None of them would ever be in a position to actually purchase my lounge. Everybody worked (and probably still does) in very safe jobs. None of them was a successful entrepreneur in his or her own right. So my question was, "Why should I even listen to any of this?"

I will tell you why. Naysayers were everywhere. All their negativity polluted my brain and I started to doubt myself. This is what happens if you listen to the same negative, or for that matter, positive message often enough, you start believing it. I couldn't help but ask myself, is my personality (i.e. determined, friendly, helpful, open minded, fun) starting to haunt me? Am I being punished for making a success out of a dump?

Of course, I knew Strawberry Lounge was built and became a success because of my personal involvement. All great companies start off as a vision of one or several courageous individuals. What normally happens is the founder moves into the background, replaces himself and works on the business. He or she will hire fabulous individuals to help run operations and expand the original business idea.

As you know, I didn't do any of this. At the end of the day it all comes down to personal preferences of what you want to do with your business. Do you want global expansion and world recognition of your name? Or rather build a "cult" establishment within your niche market?

Whoever buys the lounge had to know, it will never be the same again. But why should it? It will be different; it will be better. We needed someone who wanted to cash in on the original idea (family-oriented); who wanted to take over a success formula but not be afraid of the ghost from previous years.

I needed someone who was willing to work hard and was ready to leave his or her own mark and personal touches at the lounge. We wanted and needed someone with a big dream.

It wasn't for lack of interest that it took over a year to complete the sale. There was always an issue with potential purchasers. It was either lack of funding, lack of vision or lack of self-belief. At one point I engaged in the help of an agency but they couldn't find me a perfect match either. After a year and a few ill attempts later we found the perfect fit.

Richard and Linda walked into our life just the way I envisioned it. They both were guests at Strawberry Lounge before. They were familiar with the concept, products and our attitude. Both of them worked extensively in the hospitality business before (which wasn't a pre-requisite) and they knew about hard work and long hours. Most importantly, they had a dream, a vision – and the burning desire to succeed. They were a brother and sister team always hoping and wishing to operate their own restaurant one day. In short, I met my match and Linda and Richard found their location.

If you ever visit Bussum, please pop in and say hello to them both. Enjoy their magic touch, their enthusiasm, let them spoil you with a perfect coffee and indulge in one of the best cakes that side of the Atlantic.

It's not the same as it used to be, I know. It is better now – it's different. But then, if you never visited the original, how would you know? And most importantly, why would you care?

PART II

FAMILY AND BUSINESS DO(N'T) MIX

All too often we allow our children to become our excuses not to do what we have always wanted to do. For the longest time I did the same. Once I realized "my children will always need me, regardless of their age", I turned the table. What would happen if I allow my children to become my inspiration? What impact would I make on my children's lives if I showed them their mom is strong enough to follow one of her dreams? Would my family fall apart? Would my children be impressed, angry or careless about what I was about to start? Children learn by observation, so if this is the case, what kind of impact would I leave on my children's lives and upbringing?

In the second part of the book I will share with you what I learned about mixing family with running my own business.

Do you want to know what it takes to raise a family and a business at the same time? Are you ready for the secret? You need a fabulous spouse.

Let me elaborate on the word fabulous for a paragraph or two. Your husband (partner) should be 150% behind you. He has to support you, emotionally and even perhaps financially. At this stage in your life you can't, and don't want to, have a nagger around. You don't need somebody who doubts and second-guesses you. You need your partner to believe in you and to say: "Go Girl, I believe in you. What can I help you with?"

We need hugs, kisses, somebody who massages our feet, somebody we can chat with, somebody who is interested in our daily stories, and somebody who can drive and cook. We need somebody who can pick up the kids from soccer and can drop them off to birthday parties. The person we need wears a superman/superwoman cloak.

The moment you kiss your limiting excuses good-bye, the moment you sign the rental contract, the moment you open your doors for business is the day you kiss your well-balanced lifestyle good-bye.

In the first few months, or even years, as a new business owner there is no balance. If you think you can do it all by yourself, keep on dreaming. Of course, you can do it all but be willing to pay the price.

I tried it, and yes, I paid the price. My ego was so big. I wanted to be the perfect wife, mother, housewife, and successful businesswoman all in one and all at the same time. I failed miserably. Buying into the whole concept of multi-tasking, being multi-talented, fitting it all in, mothers doing it all? This kind of thinking sucks. There is no balance. If you try to be perfect in all categories you will go crazy.

My priorities were my business. Always and everyday from Day One onwards.

Dropping my boys off to soccer training? Puh. I rushed and rushed to make it happen. School trips with the boys? You are dreaming. Let somebody else drive. I am making coffee. Saturday morning soccer matches? I have a High Tea to cater for. Dinner invite with friends? Sorry, Dominic, you can go alone. I am tired. Play time with the kids? Sorry, have to write my shopping lists and order forms. Dropping the boys off at birthday parties? Sweetheart, can you please do that?

Exercising? Not more than twice a week, maximum (thankfully, somebody introduced me to Yoga during my start up time).

What was the worst time of the day? For me it was dinnertime. If Dominic was late home from work, I had to cook again. All day long I was making bagels, cooking eggs, serving coffees. I cleaned, vacuumed, wiped tables, cleaned and tidied up then as soon as I came home I had to do it all over again.

Sometimes I remembered to create a meal plan for the whole week. Most of the times we raided the freezer for hidden, nutritious gems.

We never had an au-pair girl. I refused to get a domestic helper. (My "logical" thinking was, I am German. I can do it better, faster and more efficiently than anyone else. Cleaning is not wasting my time. It is making me feel efficient.)

Having sex? Oh please, get real. I am in the progress of building my empire. I am focused on this one thing, and this one thing only.

Having loving, funny, encouraging conversations with my children? I believe they remember a super busy, yelling, rushing mother instead.

In other words, my social life sucked for the first year; my family went crazy for about two years.

Apparently, Sir Richard Branson had a fabulous relationship with his children throughout his whole career. How did he do it? When I meet him I will ask him. I believe his wife had something to do with it.

How did Dominic cope during the first year of operation of "wife going crazy"?

My hard-core go-getter husband transformed himself into the perfect houseman. He became a hands-on cook, chauffeur and a highly sought-after guest at birthday parties.

His transition from office-based businessman in Amsterdam to home-based businessman made the biggest difference in our lives. It was hard not to take advantage of him and overload him with a list of household chores. It took some time on his behalf to find the right balance between doing his work at home and helping out with household duties.

My relationship to our guests flourished; my relationship to my children was at times, on the rocks. Instead of giving them cuddles and bear hugs, I pushed them out the door, yelled at them, left them alone, snapped at them and I neglected them. For what? To make my dream and my vision come true.

How are our kids today? Did I scar them mentally? Are they still calling me mom? What do they remember from the time their mother went mental? Am I still married?

On two occasions I literally broke down in front of them. I cried my eyes out. I was so exhausted, so tired and so frustrated with my week. I put everything into my business and still, the week was slow. To make matters worse, I missed another one of our boys' school performances.

You didn't earn money, you yelled at your children and you are physically exhausted, how much further down the drain can you go? It can get worse. On top of all this you have the ongoing feeling of guilt. You feel so guilty about everything you do because you don't have the energy to be nice to your children. You believe deep down you are a terrible mother. This constant feeling of guilt ate me up. During my first year in business, I felt like the worst mother in the whole wide world.

During one of my emotional breakdowns Dominic took me in his arms, looked me in the eyes and said, "You are a fabulous mother. You show our boys passion, desire and success. You show our children that you can make a dream come true if you believe in yourself and if you are willing to work hard. Don't worry about a thing. Our boys will be fine. I am here for you and them."

All this was as bad as it sounds for the first one and a half to two years only. Now, that was the bad part of the story. There is also the good part.

After my whirlwind romance with setting up and starting S.L., I fell into a routine. As soon as this routine was more or less established, our life became so much easier. Eventually my staff was so good they didn't need me at the shop anymore. That was hard. I could relax but didn't want to – remember, I am a control freak.

With an established routine, my free time came back. During certain weeks I could even pick and choose if or when I wanted to run the coffee shop.

Right from the start, I made the promise never to skip our family vacation during the summer break. How hard could it be to control the business via the Internet? I went on holidays all right but was it relaxing? For the rest of the family it was. For me it was torture. My business was miles away from me and I had no control over what went on there. The girls reported to me on a daily basis, still, it was different not to be there. (Strawberry Lounge was closed Easter Sunday, Christmas and New Years Day only because I wanted continuity.)

Eventually I came to a point where I said to myself, "Stuff it Christina. Be proud of what you created, trust the girls, and go out and enjoy yourself a bit more."

The business was making money. I paid myself a bit more every month and finally I allowed myself to leave my second home more often.

During the quiet time of S.L., I left my staff alone and went for a much needed run, went swimming or went out shopping for nice, unnecessary things. Our holiday trips became more adventurous e.g. we went snorkeling in Egypt or went swimming with sharks in South Africa.

Our children found their own way of coping with their mother. Remember, children are very adaptable. Our oldest son was the first to notice the advantages of his absent mother:

- Absent mother = less supervision.
- Less supervision = less chance to get caught getting into trouble.
- Absent mother = more disposable income.
- More money to spend = less whining from mother at cash out.
- More money to spend = nicer trips.
- Verdict on having an absent mother = Not bad at all.
- Absent mother = Daddy was still around and he has always been so much more fun than mom.

Nobody can turn back the clock. Nor is it possible to make up for lost time. Hopefully, the memories our children choose to keep are happy ones like bringing their friends along for a free lunch, eating ice cream on the terrace or just passing by to give me a kiss and ask for extra pocket money.

As soon as the business made more money I allowed myself to sleep in on certain Sundays, took the afternoons off to be with the boys and enjoyed a warm glow of self-pride. Life was still busy but so much more relaxed. As soon as I knew S.L. was making money a big burden lifted off my shoulder.

There s absolutely nothing better than being in charge of your own destiny. You are your own boss, you grow as a person, and you have so much fun on a day-to-day basis that it's ridiculous. There is always the small stuff you need to get on with, for example, one of the staff called in sick at the last minute; you didn't receive the right amount of cakes and bagels; the heater broke down; the health inspector showed up (always at the busiest time); or one of your children had an accident. One afternoon our middle son cycled home alone from school and ran into a light pole. When the paramedic called me I trusted my two guests with my key and told them to lock up S.L. after they finished and leave the key with one of our neighbours.

All in all, my time as motherpreneur was fabulous. It still makes my heart jump with joy that Strawberry Lounge still exists under the new guidance of Linda and Richard. I have left a legacy, that in itself, is the best feeling ever.

My business impacted and resonated with lots of other people. I made a difference in another person's life. I utilized my unique talent to create an amazing business and I created memories for everybody who ever visited S.L. Isn't that what life is all about?

MY PARTNER DOESN'T SUPPORT ME.

I would never suggest you choose between your partner or your lifelong dream. From my personal experience, I know it takes two to tango; the two of you have to be in it together if you want to achieve something out of the ordinary.

There are many reasons why your partner doesn't see and value a project like you do. For one, it is your vision and not his. You are excited, he isn't. You want to get the bank loan; he needs to be the guarantor. You see bright lights; he only sees a dark abyss.

Men, by nature are problem solvers. Show your man you mean business. Show him you have a well thought through plan and act upon it. Show him results!

For these reasons it is worth it to re-evaluate your big dream. You might want to tweak it to accommodate your partner. I am pretty sure the two of you will figure it out.

Furthermore, a husband normally only complains if he doesn't get his needs fulfilled. So, can you still fulfill them? If not, give plenty of warning ahead of time.

Sometimes though, a woman has to put her foot down and insist on reconnecting with her own ambition. And sometimes it is time to move on. Here is one question to consider. Ask yourself: "In twenty years time when I look but at my life, will I regret not having done this?"

MY CHILDREN ARE TOO SMALL. THEY NEED ME.

Of course they need us. We need to allow our children and ourselves to enjoy the magic of motherhood. We need to give our children the security that mom will be there. However, we can easily fall into the ongoing trap of allowing our children to become our permanent excuse.

As soon as we gave birth, we became mothers. We are mothers for life. We are here to guide, to protect, to educate and inspire our children.

You will always be a mother and your children will always need you in one way or another over the course of their lives.

Our children will take us as their role model, if we want to or not. Do you want your children to follow in your footsteps? Do you consider your children as the new, courageous leaders of the future?

We all want our children to become healthy, happy, respectful citizens of the world. We as parents can only encourage them and teach them our own ways of what we think is right or wrong. And the risk is always there that our way will backfire.

We can't get it right when it comes to combining motherhood with our jobs or our own personal passions. Consider this:

- If we are not working, we feel guilty for not contributing to paying our household bills.

- If we are working, we feel guilty for leaving the kids alone.

- If we are working part-time, we are so stressed fitting everything else into our remaining free days.

- If we are working part-time, a high percentage of our wage goes towards childcare.

- If we have a top executive position we earn lots of money, however might not feel happy, and/or fulfilled.

Oh, the joys and guilty feelings of motherhood. What I am really suggesting is this: If we want or have to work and we have to leave our children in the care of a third person, wouldn't it make more sense to pursue something we really want to do? If you believe you have to feel guilty for leaving your children why not at least feel guilty following your own course?

HELP, NO BABYSITTER AT HAND

We had a few babysitters for the rare occasions we went out during the evening. We never had somebody to stay with the boys in the afternoon. Consequently, I left our children home alone quite a few times. You see, my routine for the afternoon went like this:

I picked up the boys at 3:15 p.m. from school and cycled home with them. Depending on circumstances I stayed home or left to get back to S.L. Quite often I received a phone call from my poor Strawberry girl saying, "Help, could you please come back? The lounge got invaded. I can't cope with the influx of visitors."

I hopped on my bike and cycled back as fast as I could. My boys had to keep themselves happy until Dominic came home. Man, I felt guilty leaving them. Still, I was proud my coffee shop was busy.

One afternoon, I came home late to find that our middle son Cohnan had cut Cruz's beautiful blond locks off. That was one of the moments I didn't know whether to cry or to laugh. It was bad enough they used my scissors but Cruz's beautiful curls? What went wrong there?

Apparently, they watched Disney's Snow White and the Seven Dwarfs. Our sons felt so inspired by the witch they wanted to create their own witch potion, adding real hair to the drink.

PEOPLE STEALING FROM ME

Yes, people will steal from you, or, at least, they'll try. Regardless of what kind of business you start, there is always the minority who is going to take advantage of you. That is part of business life. As far as I remember, none of my Strawberry staff cheated or stole from me. I had a few guests who, accidentally, walked out without paying. However, everybody came back immediately after they realized they had run off without paying. It was what I called, "an honest mistake". We both were talking so much and were so busy sharing our stories that I forgot to charge and she, to pay.

The one person who screwed me was my next-door neighbour.

He persuaded me to let him run a tab. He paid his first invoice after four months. This was the first warning sign that I ignored being the naïve, new businesswoman that I was.

To this day he owes me 379.00 Euro ($492) in consumed goods from S.L. Let me tell you how his twisted mind worked when I confronted him.

"Hi Joe (not his real name), how can I trust you again if you don't pay your bills. I want to think of you as an honest person but how will I know that you are not in the business of tricking me?"

Here is his reply: "Christina, you accuse me of ripping you off and you believe I am a con artist. Now I feel like I don't want to pay you at all."

Can you believe this guy?

To paint a picture, please let me break down the amount (379.00 Euro). My neighbour never paid for either

210 black coffees or

126 lattes or

152 servings of toasties (melted cheese) or

63 portions of perfectly scrambled eggs.

WHY SHOULD I GO FOR IT?

What am I most proud of? What were the biggest perks during my business life?

I was able to create my vision and the community accepted it. Strawberry Lounge was a profit-making enterprise and I could sell it under the same name. To tell the truth, it was much more than that.

The biggest reward for me was the honour of becoming part of the daily routine for so many fantastic individuals from all walks of life. I had the great pleasure and privilege to be introduced to their immediate family, to their loved ones. We shared our stories, good or bad. We hugged, we laughed, we cried together. The babies, breast-fed on the terrace turned into toddlers then into school children (school in the Netherlands starts at age four). Watching children grow up in front of your eyes makes for special bonding.

WOULD I DO IT AGAIN?

You bet I would. The whole creation process is madness. The planning, the set-up, the nerve-wracking uncertainties, the adrenaline rushes and the pride of seeing your own vision become a reality is just fantastic. Furthermore, the many wonderful, helpful - or not so helpful - people you meet along the way, are all worth it.

It is challenging to create a bond with new people in your life. It is even more fun to find out how your new guests react to your personality and in my case, over-the-top, mannerisms.

For me it wasn't about making a million bucks. (Remind me of this statement after I've earned my first mill.) It was not about brewing a state of the art coffee. It was not about making the perfect bagel spread or serving a mouth watering authentic cheesecake. What mattered most was the root of my motivation.

Strawberry Lounge was created by a mission from the heart; not by intellect, nor by business greed or by following rules. I unknowingly broke every single rule there is for a hospitality business. I just followed my heart on every decision and damned the consequences.

You just never know, one day I might serve you in my beach cafe. As I mentioned earlier, the hut and the beach really left an indelible impression on me. They both found a rent-free spot in my head. Will this ever change? I don't know. For the moment we will stay put here in Canada. If I start another Strawberry Lounge my plan needs an adaptation again. Vancouver has some wonderful spots for outdoor cafes but their beaches are nothing what I have in mind. So the big question I have to ask myself is, will I "settle for less" again? Or move to Hawaii? I will promise to keep you posted.

Thank you, Strawberry Lounge. You were my journey into self-discovery. You showed our children they mother can fly – after she decided she could.

When I stopped dreaming and got my butt into gear the story of Strawberry Lounge was an empty book. Today it is a story with a happy ending.

And what is the moral of the story? We never know how the story ends until we read to the very last page. We will never know if and how our dreams turn out if we never put our effort in to make them happen.

How will we ever know if we never try? How can we look back onto our life and not say, "I wish I had...?" We need to trust, believe and take the plunge. Only then we will ever know.

HELP IN A NUTSHELL

Kiss your excuses goodbye:

I don't have enough time.

Restructure your life (please go to www.themotherpreneur.com to upload your free worksheets of "How to create blog time" and consequently more time).

I don't have enough money.

Find an investor, borrow money from family members, make personal sacrifices, start saving, get a bridge job or a second job (www.themotherpreneur.com for more information).

My partner doesn't support me.

Go and change your husband or your dream – or forget about your dream and stick with your husband.

My children are too small.

Kids are very adaptable. If you don't want to leave them with day care or a nanny, postpone your dream and make sure you won't use your kids ages as an excuse – because they will always need you.

I don't have any experience.

Did you just read my story? Become an expert right now. Learn while doing the job. Or get qualified first.

I don't want to embarrass myself.

Who cares? Nobody. As long as you give 150% of your effort there is nothing to be ashamed of.

It is not the right time yet.

Guess what. There will never be the right time. Ever. The best time is now.

I am too old.

Get out of here. You are never, ever too old to learn, experience or do anything new in your life.

REFERENCES:
A CHECKLIST FOR SUCCESS

You should ask yourself these questions.

- Look at your bank statements: Is it in the black or in the red?
- Are your employees and suppliers paid on time?
- Can you pay yourself and still have money left over for emergencies?
- Does your business have brand or name recognition in the area?
- Do third parties refer business to you?
- Can you leave your business in the capable hands of a third party? If yes, will your enterprise still operate successfully and profitable?
- Are you happy with what you created?
- Can you sell your creation?

Depending on your answer you either have a success or failure at hand.

WORDS OF WISDOM

Looking back, it seems as if a higher power was in force with me. Being older, becoming a mother and having lived in several countries made me a much more confidant person. Yes, with age comes wisdom, you build up the right to have an opinion because you have been there and done things. You have a vision and hopefully, you are ready to fight for what it takes to make it happen. In hindsight, I am glad I made it happen when it happened.

Any kind of business thrives on relationships, some more than others. The hospitality industry is a prime example where you need to have fantastic people skills to create and stay in business. More important than the deals we make are the relationships we create with others. More important than the prices we negotiate with suppliers is our relationship we build with them. Do we trust and respect each other?

Having a good relationship with the landlord, the banker, the suppliers, the accountant, our neighbours, our employees and most importantly, our guests ensures that we have a business that runs smoothly.

One of my favourite shows is the English version of "The Apprentice". Courtesy of Lord Sugar I heard him saying: "Personality opens doors, character keeps it open." Come to think of it, how often did I get pitched by a super-friendly, enthusiastic supplier who wanted to sell and hook me on something new (e.g. a new vitamin drink, a pre-baked waffle variety to be sold as freshly baked)? Was he still as friendly and enthusiastic when I complained or stopped ordering from him?

The same counts for us as owners. Decide early on who you are and what you stand for. For example, I am a very impulsive person. I don't like to say no, I talk faster than I can think. Even now, at an age where I should know better, I still do it. These habits cost me many sleepless hours and many more awkward moments. It doesn't need to be that way. Slowly but surely, I am learning to say no. Now more than ever I ask myself, "Can I keep the promise before I say yes?" Or do I make the commitment just to look good and later come up with a lame excuse not to do it? It is so simple, really. If you can't keep your end of a deal or a promise, don't make it.

Set examples for your workforce - e.g. don't talk behind someone's back. Never, ever talk about one of your guests in front of another guest. Don't slam the competition either because walls have ears. Everything said will come back to haunt you eventually.

Remember these old sayings: "The fish stinks from the head down". And, "What goes around comes around". There is a reason why we still use them. They have both stood the test of time.

You can't be liked by everybody. This is nothing to worry about, it's just the way it is. But our actions and the way we communicate have to be liked. In business, communication and actions need to be friendly and appropriate. Follow this rule and everything will be fine. Donald Trump, eat your heart out but I never had to hire a lawyer but then I also never made a billion dollars.

For twenty years I had a personal mentor living with me. Ignored for the longest time, I finally come to appreciate the many tidbits and wise words of my own father. When I was much younger he told me, "Don't burn any bridges, and always leave a good impression, because you will always meet twice. It may be under much different circumstances but you will meet again."

"The business world is smaller than you think," he told me. Come to think of it, all areas of commerce are small. I was amazed at how many of my guests were connected and related to one another. (In Bussum it appeared that everyone knew of each other in one way or the other.)

And another good one from my father is, "People are people; it doesn't matter where you are or what you do. We all want to be treated with respect and we need somebody to listen to us."

MORE TIPS ON HAND

Conventional wisdom, as well as recent studies, has concluded that it takes 10,000 hours to master a task. Therefore we can't take short cuts. We need to put in the time to master our challenges.

Find out all the information you need to know before you get started. Find out about licenses, laws, by-laws and qualifications needed to operate the business.

Whatever your business idea is, make sure you know about any stipulation on behalf of the property. Check out the requirements by law in regards to ventilation, washrooms, health and safety, recycling, or disposing of dangerous products, just to name a few.

Take your time and read the fine print in the rental contract thoroughly. I was charged 1000.00 Euros by William because I ended the rental contract earlier than what I signed for. He conveniently disregarded the fact that Linda and Richard took over the contract with no lapse of rental income on his behalf.

Check out what the landlord allows you to do on and with his property. William didn't allow any deep-frying after Le Pierrot ceased to exist. Most probably he didn't want to pay the extra insurance premium.

Do you know what the hidden costs are? Think of newspaper and magazine subscriptions, music licenses, insurance premiums, terrace use or costs to advertise.

When I mention cost of advertising, I not only refer to printed ads in newspapers or flyers. Please be aware that some municipalities will charge for the size of logos you put on your window or on a billboard outside the shop to advertise your business.

Three years into the business, Bussum introduced this new payment for ads on our shop front. Depending on the size of your letters and display the annual costs were anything between 175.00 to 1000.00 Euro ($213-$1220). During the set-up phase, I came across a huge, plastic strawberry in a grocery store. It was the perfect piece of advertising for my coffee lounge. For this unique piece of advertisement and the fact that my strawberry stickers on the shop window were quite big, the municipality charged me 475 Euro ($579.50) per year.

Think about the existing infrastructure: What is it like? Does a public transport system exist or do local residents rely on their own transportation? If parking is available, how many spaces are available, is it free or paid parking? What are the costs and time limits?

Get in touch with the local community, e.g. music schools or any other kind of performing art school. Most students are happy to perform for free as long as they have an audience. From experience speaking, the groups I engaged were very talented.

For any kind of paint jobs try to get apprentices. They are much cheaper than fully qualified painters and offer the same quality (to an untrained eye).

If you don't have the magic touch when it comes to colour coordination, find help in colour charts. They make it easy to find out which colours will work together, which ones will have a soothing or calming effect or which ones will make your visitors hyper.

The vision is in your own head. Try to be involved in every step of the set-up phase. Nobody can do it the way you see and imagine it.

If you know any connectors, make sure they know your story. Let them spread the word.

If you have an idea in your head and for some reason have consistently postponed your "launch date", remember the following: There is no such thing as perfect timing or the right condition to start an enterprise. The right time is always now. The perfect conditions will never be perfect. Otherwise, you can wait forever.

IN CLOSING

I'm convinced that being older made me a better, nevertheless, still naïve, businesswoman. I also learned that my advanced age and life experiences gave me an edge in coping with daily business decisions. On the other hand, I was still that twenty-three year-old with her big dream running around in her bikini, serving cocktails and flirting with all the handsome bare-chested hunks, with her all time favourite music group, ABBA, blaring in the background. I'm convinced that it was for this reason and this reason only that I could relate to all the teens that flocked into The Strawberry Lounge.

With great interest I listened to their daily life worries, struggles, concerns, music and fashion trends. As a mother of future teenagers, this was all very helpful information to me. My status as a mother helped me to enjoy fun conversations with other parents about child rearing and survival strategies.

It has been a pleasure putting this book together. I can only hope that these pages have encouraged and entertained you. The Strawberry Story was written with the intention to give helpful advice to budding entrepreneurs and to offer ideas to spice up an existing business.

Strawberry Lounge is the story of Christina; it is a reflection of my personality and my character.

We all have something unique within us. I encourage you to FIND IT - USE IT and GO FOR IT, whatever it is you are planning on doing and successfully excused yourself from doing.

Don't worry what people might say about it. Life is too short for second hand opinions.

Once again, thank you for taking the time to read through these pages.

From me to you, I wish you success and best wishes along your journey.

Spread your wings; angels can fly anytime - they don't need to wait for Christmas.

HERE IS THE NITTY GRITTY BIT: HOW I SET UP MY BIZ

I registered my future business. You can register a business either as a company or as a proprietorship.

Even without a trading name or a location the clerk registered me as a "Coffee lounge in preparation" under my own name and home address. Why did I do it? Since becoming a mother I like to be prepared for any unforeseen circumstances. You never know when you might meet a future supplier. If you have a registered business you look legitimate, professional and you will be taken seriously when making enquiries.

Second: Find a good, local accountant. Local is the key here. Sometimes you need to speak to your accountant in person so being close by is key.

Let Google work for you. Call several companies up and compare prices for their services. Be very clear what you need. Nowadays you can do your own online accounting too.

Third: I needed a payroll company. I had to figure out how to employ my future employees. Should I do the pay slips myself, should I be the employer or should I hire a payroll company?

Employment rules and regulations in the Netherlands are extensive. Due to our limited understanding of the laws, it made sense to get engaged with a payroll company. The company was in charge of employing and paying for my employees. I could choose an applicant and decide on an hourly rate, the rest was up to the company. There was a price tag attached to this service. It was not cheap but as a novice to business and a foreigner with limited understanding of Dutch law, this was a small price to pay for peace of mind. Once again, it was easy to find information on Google. Do your homework; compare services and prices.

THE BUSINESS PLAN

How do I write one?

With a registered business on paper I write my business plan. A business plan is for you and for the bank (if needed) to prove that every angle of the business has been thought through properly. In most cases you will complete a business plan first before anything else happens. Don't ask me why but I did it the other way round. And yes, I was clueless on what a business plan looks like or how it is put together. Fortunately, my new best friend Google delivered the information needed as soon as I pushed the "enter" button. All you have to do is make necessary adjustments and fill in your own numbers.

Here are a few Google addresses for you to check out:

http://www.entrepreneurmag.co.za/advice/sample-business-plans/restaurants-and-bars/coffee-shop-business-plan/

http://www.youtube.com/watch?v=X3A3xR2QZvA

http://www.growthink.com/businessplan/help-center/how-to-start-a-coffee-shop (3 mistakes to avoid)

Free downloads: http://freepdfdb.org/
pdf/a-sample-business-plan-for-a-coffee-shop

With a template at hand it should have been easy but no, there were still many questions I didn't have the answers to. For example:

How do I predict a certain profit?

How long would it take before my business breaks even or makes a profit?

Does the profit vary from season to season?

How much money does a coffee bar make anyway?

What are the best ways to advertise?

How much money would I need to keep me afloat during the first year? (Unfortunately, many businesses fail during their first year in operation.)

How much money do I need to pay myself?

I had all these questions and no real answers. To get closer to the truth of the matter I visited one of our friends who is a financial wizard. I gave him the average prices for cake and coffee (3,00 and 4,00 Euros respectively) and he did the rest. We also estimated a fifty square meter floor space for the future enterprise. Furthermore, I had to decide how many tables and chairs would be available.

A wizard can only do the magic if he has all the answers to his questions. He kept on asking for more information. For example, how many hours would the coffee bar be open per day/week/month? What are the fixed costs on a monthly basis (rent, music licenses, garbage collection, telephone, gas, electricity, supplies, employment costs, and my own wage)?

For the sake of the calculations I made up amounts for many of these areas. With these numbers our friend calculated how much one of my visitors had to consume to break even, or to make an amount of 250.00, 500.00 or 750.00 Euro per day ($325, $650 or $975). Our wizard also calculated how many minutes one visitor was allowed to occupy a chair for. Of course, this was all technical and theory-based information only but at least I had some idea about how much to sell on any given day.

If none of your friends work in "wizardry", make assumptions. Go and visit lots of cafés in your neighbourhood. Drink, eat and be merry but most of all, write down different prices for their various products. Call estate agents and enquire about the prices for a rental property.

To my relief, my new Canadian acquaintances shared their hands-on experiences with me. They filled me in on how many shots of espresso I would get out of one kilo coffee. They also told me the secret of how much money it costs to serve a black coffee, to create a latte, a cappuccino or a latte with syrup shot. Surprise, surprise. As a customer it will make your eyes water when you find out how little it costs to make a decent caramel macchiato. We as owners on the other hand are rubbing our hands together with joy. The profit margin is huge.

You can say what you want about Starbucks, love them or hate them but they paved the way forward for all of us independent coffee shop owners around the world. Thanks to the giant we can get away with charging more money than necessary for the most common commodity in the world.

THE ABC'S OF STRAWBERRY LOUNGE

During my last two weeks as the owner, in December 2011, I left a farewell book for our guests. Everybody who wanted could leave our family a message.

By far the most creative note has to be the following:

The ABC's of Strawberry Lounge

Action

Body Beautiful (our mixed drink: O-juice, banana, strawberries)

Coffee the way we like it/Cheesecake/Canada

Daily Delights

Energy

Fun

Genuine

Hot ladies in the service

In between going shopping

Join us

Kick-start (another mix drink: o-juice & banana)

Laughter

More of the same

Not to be missed

Oven fresh muffins

Pioneer

Quick caffeine fix

Romance under the mistletoe

Super Service

Top Team

Unique spot in Bussum

Very Valued

We will miss you

Xtra-ordinary large piece of cake

Young at heart

"Zee" you in Canada

BIBLIOGRAPHY

The only business book I read before opening Strawberry Lounge was:

Hashemi, Sahar and Bobby "Anyone Can Do It" England, Capstone Publishing Ltd. 2002

These are the business related books I read after I regained my sanity:

Dennis, Felix "How to get Rich", England, Ebury Press 2006

Godin, Seth "Purple Cow", USA, Portfolio (Penguin Books) 2002

Schultz, Howard & Yang, Dori Jones, "Pour your Heart into It", USA, Hyperion 1997

Printed in Canada